IDENTITY THEFT

Victim

Help & Support
After The Crime

Agony & Answers…Trauma to Triumph

By

LouAnn Busch-White

ISBN: 1-4033-5755-2 (e-book)
ISBN: 1-4033-5756-0 (Paperback)

Library of Congress Control Number: 2002093528

This book is printed on acid free paper.

Printed in the United States of America
Bloomington, IN

1stBooks – rev. 10/9/02

This book is dedicated to my parents and my husband whose constant love and never ending support, encouragement and understanding through my identity theft ordeal, gave me the strength to fight my injustice.

Contents

Acknowledgment vii

Notation   ix

Introduction: *Why Read This Book?* xi

Chapter 1   What is Identity Theft and How Did I

Catch It? 1

Chapter 2   Your New Job: CEO of "Getting My

Identity Back Incorporated" 3

Chapter 3   What Personal Information Do Thieves

Want & How Do They Get It? 10

Chapter 4   Identity Theft Agony: Trauma I & II 33

Chapter 5   Being Victimized Changes You 42

Chapter 6   Things I Bet You Didn't Know 50

Chapter 7   The Scary Part: It's Out There and It's

Waiting for You! 56

Chapter 8   The 3 C's: 64

Chapter 9   Quiz to Determine Your Vulnerability 69

Chapter 10 Ways to Help Minimize Your Vulnerability 73

Chapter 11 Turning Procrastination into

Perseverance: Creating Your System 82

Chapter 12 Disputing Unauthorized Information

Appearing on Your Credit Reports.................... 110

Chapter 13 Overview of Some of Today's Frauds and

Scams... 117

Chapter 14 Some Pertinent Laws that Might Help

You... 131

Chapter 15 Important Organizations and Contacts......... 139

Chapter 16 Sample Letters.. 142

Conclusion 164

Acknowledgment

I would like to acknowledge a company that has played a very special role in helping make this book possible. I extend my inexpressible gratitude to Oxygen Media, a company that truly believes in the power of women to make a difference. Oxygen's belief that Identity Theft Management™ and I could help make a difference in the lives of the estimated 800,000 annual identity theft victims gave me the courage to write a book I hope you find informative and empowering.

Notation

My intention was to write a book offering information, support and guidance to the staggering numbers of victims of identity theft who want the opinions of a fellow victim, need to know they are not alone, need more information about the crime of identity theft and want insight and help into ways they can try to prove their innocence and victim status to merchants, creditors, collection and credit reporting agencies regarding fraudulent debts and activity preformed in their name. Certain actions performed in the identity theft victim's name or placed against the victim may require contacting an attorney or a member of the legal profession. Legal actions such as judgments, liens, warrants, etc. should ALWAYS be referred to a member of the legal profession for advice and counsel as soon as they become known. This book was not written as a *legal* guide. It should not be construed as legal advice. All legal questions and guidance should always be directed to an attorney or a member of the legal profession. Those actions are beyond the scope of this book and its author and will not be considered or addressed.

This book and its content are provided "as is" without any warranties. This book and the author make no guarantees expressed or implied. This book and the author make no representations regarding the guarantee of regaining credit worthiness, personal information or stolen identity. In no event shall the author be liable for any direct, consequential, incidental, special, punitive or other damages whatsoever as it relates to the content of this book. The entire risk arising out of any opinions expressed and suggestions followed remains with the reader. Any deletions, errors or omissions found are made without intent or malice.

Introduction

I wrote this book for the many victims of identity theft that feel a *violation* that often can't be expressed because too many people still don't understand the severity of this crime. These are usually people who haven't been *personally* affected and don't know the destruction, havoc and trauma inflicted on its victims; victims who too frequently, find themselves alone in the battle to regain their identity from an often-unknown assailant. I wrote this book to share needed information about an overwhelming, frustrating and time-consuming crime. I wrote this book because too many identity theft victims struggle daily to prove their innocence and victim status in a confusing "guilty until proven innocent" system. Too many don't understand their rights when it comes to credit information and inaccuracies. Too many victims believe their circumstances must be unique because not many people understand or seem to know how to help. Too many victims find themselves victimized twice, once by their impostor and then again by the present system. Nothing and no one seems to be stopping or even slowing this crime's dangerous escalation. Not many people grasp the devastating repercussions or the legacy it leaves on its victims. When victims do receive help, it's too often ineffective, unspecific and capitulatory. I want to reach people weighed down by the ineffective advice, the vague responses and the no solution attitudes. There is a big difference in seeking advice from large agencies designed to handle hundreds or thousands of calls and advice from victims that have gone before you. I am one of those victims who not only understands what you are going through but have dedicated myself to working and advocating on behalf of the estimated 800,000 identity theft victims annually.

There is no simple answer to the question so many people ask about how I successfully regained my identity. It was hard work. It wasn't easy. It was tedious and it was time-consuming.

But in the end, I was successful. Whenever, I have only brief moments to explain my accomplishment, I always share the fact that I only began to achieve success when I turned my debilitating panic and its accompanying procrastination in facing the problem head on...into unrelenting *perseverance*. I stopped being so overwhelmed and *persisted* in getting people to h-e-a-r me.

I also wrote this book for all those people who think it won't happen to them. Knowing what this crime really entails, I get annoyed when I read all the little "suggestions and tips" for protecting one's identity. All the misleading information provided to consumers that, if followed, will "*prevent*" them from becoming victims. What happens when it doesn't work? What happens when the lists of tips aren't enough? What happens when the crime of identity theft has become so widespread, so pervasive that it is unmanageable, often undetectable, and virtually unavoidable? What happens to the people that follow every suggestion ever printed...but thieves steel their identity anyway? It's disappointing when organizations, associations and agencies lead consumers to believe that if they just follow the list of do's and don'ts, they won't fall victim to this devastating crime. Don't feel guilty if, or when, it happens to you. What they fail to tell you in all their many lists of Do's and Don'ts is that you can follow every suggestion to "*prevent*" identity theft and still become victimized! What they don't tell you is that we have surpassed the **"*preventing*"** stage of this crime. You can do things to try to "minimize" your chances of becoming a victim. You can alter your behavior to try to lessen your vulnerability but *prevent*, not any more! Identity theft is the fastest growing crime in America. Why? One answer is the ease in which personal information is obtained and then duplicated. Add to that the crime's potentially high payoff compared to the low risk of apprehension. It is time we recognize and then deal with the real problems this crime presents. We need a lot more than new laws that make it easier to prosecute identity thieves. Most victims wonder who would be prosecuted anyway? Who *ARE* these criminals?

Where are they? How many law enforcement officers would it take to track them down? Laws are good and laws are necessary but laws alone haven't made a dent in stopping these unlawful people. In addition to laws other things MUST change. We MUST stop making our personal information so readily available. We must alter the way we process credit cards if the thieves have mastered the process too. We must think of enhancements or alternatives to identification cards such as our driver license and social security card when we find that thieves have easily mastered their duplication. We must stop using the social security *number* as our main identification number before it becomes so compromised that it's totally ineffective. We must insist on social security number privacy. There are things we can do.

The number of innocent, hard working people victimized by this often life altering crime is staggering. The problem we are facing now is a list of victims that grows exponentially each year. Sadder yet, is that after becoming a victim, you will find very little real, "take-me-by-the-hand-and-help-me" kinds of assistance. Many identity theft victims are left to deal with the financial, emotional, psychological and physical effects...on their own! Until we come together and demand that our legislators help keep our personal information out of the hands of unscrupulous people, this crime will continue to explode. Until we decide that the simple series of numbers on magnetic strips on the back of credit cards is thoroughly out-dated and too easily hijacked, this crime will continue to escalate. Until we out-pace or at the least, keep pace with the criminal element, more of us will continue to be victims and our national security will be further jeopardized. If you've been victimized by identity thieves, don't feel guilty. It's no longer preventable. It's probably nothing that you did or didn't do. If you've been victimized, you can't let it spiral out of control. You must become proactive in resolving your situation. If you're a consumer in today's society, you need to be educated on the behaviors that make you vulnerable. In all cases, you need to read this book.

There are many more reasons to read this book. Read it to understand some links as to why the crime of identity theft and fraud have escalated out-of-control. Read it to understand that although we have surpassed the "prevent" identity theft stage, there ARE ways you can try to "minimize" the risks of becoming an identity theft victim. Read it to learn about ways criminals target you and what you can do to try to thwart their plans. If you are or become an identity fraud victim, it covers the all too real expectation that creditors will assume you are guilty of incurring the debts you declare fraudulent. It confirms the burden victims carry when they must consistently prove their innocence. It recognizes that creditors and collectors will contact you two, three, and four times about debts you've already notified them were unauthorized and fraudulent. It informs you of laws that protect consumers against inaccurate or erroneous credit information. It suggests a proactive and systematic plan to follow should merchants, creditors and collection agencies contact you about fraudulent activity performed in your name. It offers suggestions when creditors and credit reporting agencies *ignore* your requests pertaining to inaccurate or incorrect information. It gives you the incentive, assistance, and knowledge to try to prove your victim status and to proactively try to stop your impostor's activities.

Once read, you will be acutely aware that major changes must be made before we see a reduction in the estimated 800,000 thousand annual victims we're currently seeing. It is important to acknowledge the toll the crime of identity theft takes on our nation and its people before we can successfully fight it. We must recognize that our present societies' ineffectiveness to deal with this crime creates life altering financial, physical, emotional, and psychological hardships on every victim. Having our sensitive personal information easily accessed and illegally used has far-reaching effects in our society, our nation and the world. We were all affected by identity fraud as a result of September 11 and yet little has *really* changed. In the end, only victims can explain the very real violation this crime imposes and the ever lasting and life-altering legacy it leaves behind.

Lou Ann

Identity Theft Victim: Help and Support After the Crime
Agony & Answers…Trauma to Triumph

Chapter 1

What is Identity Theft and How Did I Catch It?

Identity theft is not a disease. You can't catch it from anyone, although it has spread as if it were contagious! Everyone seems to know someone, who has experienced it and as coincidence would have it, a mere two months after reading an article about it, it actually happened to you! Identity theft occurs when someone takes your personal information such as your name, date of birth, address or social security number without your knowledge and uses it to commit theft or fraud, stealing from you or stealing from others IN YOUR NAME. Identity theft is when someone robs your identity! It's when an impostor pretends to be you! It presently affects approximately 800,000 consumers a year with no end in site.

Now that it's happened to you, it's real. The crime you have merely read or talked about, really happens! And it has happened to you! None of the articles you read ever really explained how devastating this crime really is. No one explained how violated you feel. Furthermore, you have recounted everything you've done and wonder how thieves obtained your personal information. You didn't lose your wallet, your credit cards, your checkbook. You didn't open any new accounts, buy anything on-line or answer questions from a telemarketer. You didn't give your social security number to unknown persons, refinance your home, bank on line or have your mail stolen. You really don't consider yourself an easy target. Well, let's see. Did you write a check for anything? Did you furnish your social security number for any reason? Do you have a driver's license? Do you work? Do you have medical insurance? Do you pay taxes? Do you have a cell phone? Do you own a house? Do you have a marriage

1

license? Do you have a brokerage account? Do you vote? Do you have credit cards? Do you live in today's society?

All too often, it turns out that you didn't do anything to "catch" it. IT catches you by the sheer fact that you ARE your personal information and your personal information is everywhere. You supply personal information constantly and businesses share your personal information. Now that you have firsthand knowledge of the devastating consequences, you find yourself reluctant to share any personal information with any one for any reason. But…you must. You really have very little choice in the matter. Supplying and collecting personal information is a very real part of our society.

So, now that you know it was nothing you overtly did that brought on the nightmare you're now living, do you feel better? No? You are still left with having to deal with angry merchants, creditors, and collection agencies. Your credit report is full of inaccurate and incorrect information? You can't get a loan for that new car you've saved for or the approval to refinance your home? You've been denied the new credit cards you've applied for and you were turned down for the job you wanted? Wow, you must be depressed!

It appears that you did, in fact get a new job. Your new job requires knowledge, experience and the attributes of *perseverance* and *persistence.*

Chapter 2

Your New Job:
CEO of "Getting My Identity Back Incorporated"

You have your full-time job away from home and you have hundreds of other jobs to do when you arrive back home. The last thing you needed was another job called, "Who In The World Stole My Identity And How Do I Get It Back Incorporated!"   Believe me, it is another very full and demanding JOB! But guess what? You not only got the job; they offered you the position of CEO! The only qualities you may be lacking are both the knowledge and experience to be successful in your new position.

Let's begin the education needed to be successful in your new position as Chief Executive Officer with some basic information.   Let's make sure that you have a basic understanding of the term fraud.   Fraud simply defined is a deliberate deception practiced to secure unfair or unlawful gain; one who cheats; an impostor. Identity theft is one type of fraud. It is also referred to as identity fraud. Identity theft is when someone takes your personal information such as your name, social security number or other personally identifiable information without your knowledge and commits fraud or theft. It is the fasting growing crime in America. Well over three-quarters of a million people will become victims of this crime this year.   Why are there so many victims? There are a multitude of answers and opinions.   Although we've made identity theft a *real* crime, all too often it has very few real consequences for the perpetrators. Thieves know that the potential benefits of this crime very often outweigh the possible repercussions. Therefore, the risk is often times low and the pay-off high.

The crime of identity theft is really quite easy to accomplish. One reason for this is the tremendous amount of personal information we are required to furnish or freely make available for others to see. What specifically is *personal information*? It refers to personally identifiable information. Any name or number that may be used either alone or in conjunction with any other information to identify a specific individual. This includes personal information such as your name, your address, your maiden name, social security number, date of birth, driver's license or identification number, alien registration number, government passport number, employer or taxpayer identification number, your Medicaid or food stamp account number, financial account numbers and so on. Computer technology is another reason why identity theft is easy to accomplish today. Our technology can give almost anyone the opportunity to electronically access and duplicate personal information and they can do it virtually undetected.

Even with the tremendous growth of this crime and the incredible number of victims it claims, many people still don't understand what identity theft actually is until it happens to them. Most people that know about identity theft believe the chance of becoming it's victim is slim. In reality, if it hasn't happen to you, you've been...LUCKY. Today, you can try everything within your power to protect your personal information from getting into the public domain and the hands of unscrupulous people but as I mentioned in chapter one, if you are living in today's society, you can keep very little of your personal information private.

Your neighbor could be a victim of this crime right now and not know it. In many instances, identity theft goes undetected by its victim for months and sometimes years. A short time ago, law enforcement in California contacted one of my client's for outstanding child support payments. It seems my client's wallet had been stolen five years earlier in Florida. His wallet thief apparently got married and had children in California, a state my client had never even visited. The thief assumed my client's identity and used his name and social security number as personal identification when he wed and when his children were born. Following unyielding denials and abundant documentation, California law enforcement later discovered the real identity of the impostor and went after him for child support but had little interest in apprehending the criminal for identity theft especially when the victim lived thousands of miles away. After pleading with these authorities to apprehend his imposter for identity theft, he was informed that their paperwork only covered child support!

In your new position as CEO, it is important to become acquainted with the Federal Trade Commission and what it offers victims of identity theft. The Federal Trade Commission is the government's primary consumer protection agency. Its jurisdiction extends over nearly the entire economy, including business and consumer transactions. Part of the agency's mandate is to take action against "unfair or deceptive acts or practices." It provides information and suggests ways to help consumers identify and possibly prevent some fraudulent practices from happening. Under the Federal Trade Commission Act, the FTC has authorization to halt deception through civil actions filed by its own attorneys in federal district court, as well as through administrative cease and desist actions. After the passage of the Identity Theft and Assumption Deterrence Act of 1998 (commonly called The Identity Theft Act), the FTC set up a separate identity theft program to handle some of the difficulties victims of identity theft experience. Prior to this 1998 law, only banks and various financial institutions and creditors were considered "victims." It was widely believed that these institutions were the only ones that sustained monetary losses however, with the passing of The Identity Theft Act, consumers experiencing harm to their financial history or credit reputation were also considered victims. The FTC advises identity theft victims on steps they can take to help minimize the harm to both finances and credit. Their identity theft website, www.consumer.gov/idtheft, is easily accessible and is an excellent source for referrals, guidance, information, suggestions, phone numbers, addresses of agencies, identity theft laws, links to other useful sites and more. I always suggest all potential clients visit the FTC website prior to scheduling a consultation with Identity Theft Management. A knowledgeable and enlightened client facilitates attaining the desired goals. Additionally, the FTC has created a standard Forgery Affidavit covering NEW fraudulent accounts opened in victims' names. Their affidavit is accepted by various creditors. They are actively working on a number of *standard* forms and systems to assist in proving your victimization. They are also trying to help victims by lowering the amount of calls victims must make to each of the three national credit reporting agencies, (also know as credit bureaus). The FTC, along with identity theft victims, would like to see this reduced to one call with all three national credit reporting agencies notified.

In addition, the FTC's Bureau of Consumer Protection compiles various statistics from calls they receive from identity theft victims through their Consumer Response Center. This is a hot line set up for victims to report their identity theft problems. The statistical information the Bureau provides may be a little misleading because most of it is based on information supplied by victims that actually call them. Not every victim calls them. I'm a victim. I didn't call. When my identity was stolen in 1997, I didn't have the opportunity to call a consumer protection agency set up for identity theft victims yet, had I this resource, I was still not prepared psychologically to give more people information about ME. I believe many victims today feel the same way. I already felt violated. I was not ready to give information about myself to more people I didn't know, to be stored in more databases that might be seen by yet more unknown persons that might lead to further violation. (This is a large part of the psychological trauma of this crime. Psychologically, I wanted to keep private as much personal information that was within my power to keep private. Please don't think I wanted to become anonymous. Far from it. I just wanted to keep private the personal information I believed made me particularly vulnerable to further financial fraud. This is part of the legacy of this crime. You try to guard your sensitive personal information from just about everyone). Some agencies that I did contact to determine if they could help me asked for so much of my personal information that I did not finish the conversations nor did I complete any forms they mailed me. They asked me questions I was not prepared both psychologically and emotionally to answer. What were they going to do with my answers and my information anyway? Were my answers on paper documents to be disposed of without shredding once they were input into a database? Was I talking with temporary or contracted workers that had access to information they typically would not have otherwise? Was I sharing my sensitive personal information with a small company that had subcontracted this work from a larger organization? A small subcontractor that possibly held no loyalty to the values of the larger organization, had under gone no security or background verification or perhaps had little or no security or encryption devices on their computer systems! All this might sound a bit neurotic but again, this is the legacy of the crime). After they asked me the questions, I discovered that most had no in-place plan for answers. So, had I given them the personal information they requested, what were they going to do with it? In 1997, no one offered me any real answers. Today there are better systems in place along with organizations and companies that specifically help victims of identity theft through organized systems and methodologies. Government agencies like the Federal Trade Commission have designated departments to offer assistance and handle identity theft information. Much of the data collected from identity theft victims by the FTC helps support law enforcement agencies' efforts to combat identity theft. They use the collected data to spot patterns of illegal activity and to assist in identifying emerging trends and directions of identity theft in certain geographical areas. The data also helps law enforcement agencies more readily identify organized identity theft rings. Therefore, today, the importance of placing the call should not be undervalued or dismissed lightly. The phone counselors take a report and offer victims steps to follow to notify the necessary authorities and agencies of their incident. The FTC's toll free identity theft hotline is *877-IDTheft*. The FTC's Consumer Response Center also has a web-based consumer complaint database.

The Federal Trade Commission continues to evolve and advance in answer to the explosive growth in identity theft victims. Although their victims' assistance is growing and improving constantly, they are still a government agency and therefore offer help and assistance to large numbers of people. Some victims complain that the assistance is too general and is offered on a mass information basis. After contacting the Federal Trade Commission, if you find you need more individualized assistance you can always contact additional organizations and companies like mine, Identity Theft Management,™ www.identitytheftmanagement.com, that specialize in helping individual victims on a personal level. I strongly suggest all victims of identity theft begin with the information offered by the FTC by visiting their website at: www.consumer.gov/idtheft

As acting CEO of your newly formed company, you need to establish your goals and then the steps or objectives, to meet those goals. Throughout your ordeal, never loose touch with your goals. They provide the direction you need to avoid becoming overwhelmed, frustrated, angry and disappointed. For purposes of this book, I'm going to provide your two goals:

1. **Get the thieves to STOP using *your* personal information.**
2. **Prove your innocence and victim status to creditors, collection agencies and credit bureaus.** (Certain actions taken against you may require your having to contact an attorney. Legal actions such as judgments,

liens, warrants, etc., should ALWAYS be referred to your attorney or a member of the legal profession as soon as you are aware of them. Those actions are beyond the scope of this book and will not be addressed).

I have found that the best way to try to get thieves to "stop impersonating you," is to make it too uncomfortable for them to continue being you. You must try to accomplish this by setting up roadblocks, becoming proactive and by not letting your situation snowball or escalate beyond manageability. Although it is not unusual to want to ignore the situation, simply *wishing* it hadn't happened and *hoping* it just "goes away," doesn't work. Time is a critical component in your accomplishing your goals. You must learn to turn any type of reluctance or procrastination in dealing with the situation into unrelenting persistence and perseverance. Your second goal, proving your innocence and victim's status is achieved by following a systematic plan. A big part of the plan's success lies in your understanding why you must act and then following through once you do.

Now that a good foundation has been laid for you to understand the goals and the objectives in reaching those goals, let's learn more about the information required to be successful in your new job. Let's learn more about the personal information thieves want and how they get it.

Chapter 3

What Personal Information Do Thieves Want

&

How Do They Get It?

I've listed some of the information thieves want and obtain from a variety of sources. The *main* target of every identity thief however, is your SOCIAL SECURITY NUMBER. Never forget that. When your social security number or other personally identifiable information falls into dishonest hands, it may be used by someone to impersonate you in order to steal from your accounts or to steal from others in your name. I have listed some personal information that identity thieves want:

- o Your name
- o Maiden names
- o Birth date
- o Your addresses and telephone numbers
- o Your place of birth
- o Driver's license number
- o PIN numbers
- o Credit card numbers, debit card and ATM numbers
- o Pass words
- o Checking account and routing numbers
- o Employer or taxpayer identification number
- o Alien registration numbers
- o Investment account numbers
- o Medicare account numbers
- o Social Security number

Before looking at the many ways thieves get your personal information, let's look at *who* these thieves may be. Some you know and some you don't. They can be:

- o Trusted employees and co-workers
- o Temporary employees and outsourced and contracted personnel
- o Friends and relatives
- o Computer hackers
- o Telemarketers
- o Organized crime rings
- o Amateur, run of the mill thieves

There are innumerable ways thieves acquire your personal information. I have listed some.

- ➤ Digging through garbage
- ➤ Stealing mail
- ➤ Stealing checks
- ➤ Stealing unshredded bank statements
- ➤ Snatching wallets, purses, briefcases and palm pilots
- ➤ Real and phony telemarketers call you and ask and receive personal information
- ➤ From résumés and other information posted *online*
- ➤ From applications
- ➤ From Internet banking and shopping
- ➤ Taxes filed over the Internet
- ➤ Temporary, outsourced and contracted workers and dishonest employees having access to company databases can download your personal information contained in tax and personnel records, medical and credit files, etc.
- ➤ From medical information obtained from you and stored on unsecured computers
- ➤ Medical information that is transferred into computer databases from paper documents that are simply thrown in the trash without shredding

➢ Professional office computer databases that have no security or encryption devices.
➢ Dishonest employees working for merchants, restaurants, medical facilities, car dealerships and financial institutions that make extra imprints or copies of your credit card, loan documents, medical records, loan applications and rental agreements
➢ Unscrupulous people posing as landlords, employers, loan officers, real estate agents and others purchase a copy of your credit report
➢ From skimming devices, con games, legitimate credit card machines and public records
➢ Friends, relatives, ex-spouses and ex-relatives that have access to information through their relationship with you

Reading the above list can make you nauseous. Everyday I receive calls from victims shocked that someone has used their name to open a credit card account or used other identifying information such as their social security number or driver license to commit fraud in their name. As previously mentioned, many have no idea how it happened. Other common forms of identity theft include taking over an existing credit card account and making unauthorized charges on it. This is not unusual. The identity thief delays discovery by contacting the credit card issuer and changing the billing address on the account. Other thieves take out loans in another person's name. They write fraudulent checks using another person's name and/or account number. They open telephone or wireless service accounts and utility accounts in someone else's name. In some cases, the identity thief completely takes over the victim's identity. They open bank accounts, obtain multiple credit cards, buy cars, obtain home mortgages and might even work and have children under the victim's name and social security number! (Remember my client?) Identity thieves simply steal mail or "dumpster dive" through trash to collect *unsolicited* credit card offers or other identifying information such as account numbers or social security numbers. It's shocking how many people don't tear or shred their private documents. Thieves also employ more sophisticated practices. In a crime known as "skimming," identity thieves use "card readers" to read and store the information encoded on the magnetic strip on the back of your ATM, debit or credit card. Either the thief inserts your credit card through these card readers or they have compromised legitimate payment machines such as the card readers used on the gas pump at your favorite gas station or on the register at your local department store. Once your information is stored, it can be re-encoded onto any blank card with a magnetic strip, instantly transforming the blank card into a bogus ATM, debit card or credit card identical to yours! (All this is done through no fault of your own). Organized crime rings love this scam! Much of the hijacked information is skimmed and can be on its way to whatever state or country the ring operates from within seconds of your purchase. Many of the portable card readers are small enough to fit into a restaurant server's or store clerk's pocket making detection difficult and too often impossible.

Identity theft's present unmanageability along with its imperceptibility and too often unavoidability are most often due to the anonymity that computer technology offers the criminal element. Today's affordable computer technology makes the criminal opportunity available to just too many. Computers offer identity thieves and organized identity theft rings virtual absence of physical presence in pulling off their scams. Wow, consider the limitless opportunities!

I listen to hundreds of stories from both men and women who have had their identities stolen after having their wallets or purses taken. This type of crime actually accounts for a small percentage of identity fraud in America today. Today, Congress, the FBI, the Secret Service, Federal, State and Local law enforcement agencies are alarmed by the large crime rings that have sprung up and are responsible for the explosion of identity fraud throughout the country. Many fraud rings operate by recruiting inside employees working for large companies and have those dishonest employees download the companies' employee lists of names and social security numbers. The unsuspecting innocent employees' identities are then used for various fraudulent activities. The FTC has reported that incidences of workplace identity theft appear to be increasing. The Commission has reportedly received information of identity thieves compromising personnel records of hospitals, schools, and other employer's since 1999. The New York Times published the arrest of a former insurance employee who had reportedly downloaded the personal information of thousands of employees from the insurance company's database. They reported that the employee then advertised the sale of the information over the Internet.

This type of "inside job" also happens at well-known credit card companies. Three customer service representatives working at a prominent credit card company were indicted on charges of selling customer's names, addresses, telephone numbers, social security numbers and credit card expiration dates to members of an identity theft ring.

Today many, many employers use temporary or contracted workers. These workers are typically within the company for a short duration of time, usually to accomplish specific tasks or to cover seasonal needs. These employees often have access to personal information through the work they perform. Jobs like data entry, customer service, records, and other computer projects expose unscrupulous workers to opportunities in which they can make copies of personnel records, loan applications, rental agreements, medical records and employment applications and in turn, sell the information to thieves and organized identity fraud rings. These types of records are quite desirable and have a recognized street value. Many of the rings are selective and reportedly pay more for particular companies! The rings know what credit card numbers belong to which company by the first four digits of the card. They know which companies require PINs or passwords for identification and which do not. Logically, it's the credit card numbers of the companies with the least number of safeguards in place that are the most desirable by these criminals. Be sure to check with your credit card company and find out what security measures are in place to help keep you from additional exposure to financial fraud. Most financial companies are aware of the numerous schemes and tactics of these identity theft rings yet, not all employ the latest in security measures. For years, I used one particular card as my primary credit card. Often months would pass without my making a sizable or uncharacteristically major purchase with my card. On the rare occasion that I did, I can honestly say that not once in 20 years did the credit card company verify that it was actually *me* making those unusual purchases. On the other hand, when my husband purchased our wedding rings using his Discover Card, he received a call that *same* night from a Discover representative verifying that it was my (now) husband, that had in fact, charged such an unusually large amount on his card. Many people feel offended by these security actions; DON'T BE. Do you think your creditor is trying to harm you by calling? How? Do you think it's an invasion of your privacy? When they don't call and it's not you making those purchases, you quickly learn about a REAL invasion of your privacy! Don't be foolish. Demand that the credit card company you utilize verify unusual activity. It protects everyone.

According to most recent statistics offered by the Federal Trade Commission, the most common forms of identity theft are:

Credit Card Fraud - a credit card account is opened in a consumer's name or an existing credit card account is "taken over."

Communications Services Fraud - the identity thief opens telephone, cellular, or other utility service in the consumer's name.

Check Fraud - a checking or savings account is opened in the consumer's name, and/or fraudulent checks are written.

Fraudulent Loans - the identity thief obtains a loan, such as a car loan, in the consumer's name.

A few years ago an incredibly deceitful couple used the information supplied in Who's Who In America to impersonate and steal. All of the victims had been profiled in the famous directory that included biographical information such as their complete name, date of birth, place of birth, mother's maiden name and their home address. It actually gave enough information in each person's biography so that the impostors were able to request copies of birth certificates. Yet with all the information they received from the directory on each person, the deceitful couple still needed the actual social security numbers before they could open new credit card accounts. Apparently, they had little trouble obtaining these through each state's motor-vehicle department. Lying about being involved in a minor fender bender, the impostors requested a copy of each person's driving record from the states where the social security number appeared in the DMV file or on the license itself. They went on to devastate the financial histories of these credit worthy people. Although it is an honor to appear in such notable directories, it is important to remember the times in which we live. We all need to be aware of the consequences and possible danger publishing this type of personal information imposes.

As I've continued to point out, there are many, many ways thieves obtain your personal information. I'm going to touch on just six areas that I believe contribute our vulnerability in having our personal information violated.

(1) The Freedom of Information Act

The Freedom of Information Act passed in 1966, (amended in 1974 and 1986), changed the way society labeled much of what was once referred to as "private and personal" information to information that is publicly available, known as *public information*. Public information is specifically information that is created, compiled and/or maintained by the government. Society adapted quickly once personal information began being labeled as "public information," Today, most people do not believe it an infringement but rather believe, "if it's public information, we have a right to access it." Once your personal information gets into the public domain, it may be accessed by virtually anyone and is impossible to protect. The easy and anonymous access to personally identifiable information makes you very vulnerable yet, it is public information or a matter of *public record* therefore, we have a right to access it.

The Freedom of Information Act, (FOIA), specifies that the public owns the information and data that is in trust with the government on both the state and federal levels and that information is available to the people accept where restricted by law. Fortunately, the FOIA does have certain limitations and exceptions. Computer technology and the Internet however, added a whole new dimension to "freedom of information." Before the Internet, access to public records required written requests for the information signed by and identifying the requester. The Internet's easy availability and its worldwide dissemination of information made access to this public information unrestricted and anonymous and its management...impossible. The government realized that electronic public record access and its management were insecure and required regulation and guidelines. On October 2, 1996, President Clinton signed the Electronic Freedom of Information Act, or EFOIA. The primary goal of this act was to make electronic records subject to Freedom of Information Act requests. The EFOIA changed the rules with regard to accessing government information but most individual states have *not* yet instituted equivalent versions of the EFOIA, therefore there are very few restrictions to the distribution of individual state government data over the Internet.

We need to be very aware and quite concerned about the availability of government information on the Internet. In addition to thieves and organized crime rings, who else benefits from the advantages of our public (personal) information? Is it your next-door neighbor? Is it the cashier at the grocery store? Is it your kid's teacher? No, of course not. Let me ask again. Is it your mortgage broker? Is it your real estate agent? Is it your banker? Is it your insurance agent? Is it every marketer from coast to coast? Is it newspaper journalists? Gee, do you think publicly available personal information is good for b-u-s-i-n-e-s-s? Do you think corporate America uses it for marketing purposes? Of course! The average citizen does not directly benefit from making other people's personal information of public record however, business has turned it into quite a profitable venue. Try to stop some of your personal information from becoming a matter of public record. You can't. The wisdom of having personal information so easily accessed through public records must be questioned. The average American does not need such easy access to so much personal information on other average citizens. The cost of providing that information is that there are unscrupulous people and organizations that have access to your personal information and use it to harm you. The average consumer is slowly realizing that public (personal) information has the potential of causing them much more harm than good. Most businesses and journalists are quick to respond that it is in the "public's best interest" to provide access to certain public information. Let me remind you: there are approximately 800,000+ *annual* cases of identity theft from unscrupulous people using the personal information of others. And although there is no one central agency in the United States responsible for calculating how many people are victimized by this crime each year, we are able to get estimates from people reporting their victimization to law enforcement, creditors, banks, credit reporting agencies and the Federal Trade Commission. The crime has escalated so rapidly that many fear it is unstoppable. Each of the three national credit agencies is reported to be receiving 50,000+ calls from victims per month! That figure coupled with the calls received by the other agencies along with a fair estimate of those people whose victimization goes unreported would indicate that we have far surpassed 800,000 annual victims.

There are state and federal laws that increase the degree of the crime if it is determined the crime was facilitated or furthered by the use of a public record. It is good that governments realize the potential harm that can be done if the information contained in public records is misused yet, what is it really accomplishing? Will identity thieves stop using public information to commit their crimes because it's against the law and identity thieves are such law-abiding citizens? Is the risk of getting caught greater than the pay-off or reward? I understand it gives the legal process yet another vehicle for prosecution. But as mentioned, so many of these crimes are committed in anonymity so prosecution is often impossible. Yet, the damage is still done! The ability to prosecute or not, has not deterred this crime from escalating out of control let alone stopped the crime from taking place. During the investigation of the World Trade Center terrorists, it was soon suspected that the hijackers of the planes were not who we originally thought they were. It was learned that some passports and identities had been stolen and that computer technology significantly added to the ease of their crime. Were *they* prosecuted? Was the damage still done?

Prosecuted or not, ever increasing numbers of victims have an overwhelming task in front of them. Still left unanswered are the following issues:

1. Police, various law enforcement agencies, the secret service, Congress and our legal system readily admit they are overwhelmed with the staggering number of perpetrators of these crimes. Can the creation of laws alone work if the system in place to enforce the laws is *overwhelmed*?

2. We must examine more than the creation of legal rules. How high does the annual number of victims need to climb before we seriously examine the availability of public information and it's link to this catastrophic problem?

3. When laws alone don't make a dent in stopping the proliferation of this crime, the crimes' financial and economic effects become much more far reaching. What happens when an unusually high percentage of our in-place consumer credit structure is in question?

4. When the laws alone don't stop this crime, who helps the exorbitant numbers of victims that require a lot more than the cursory help they are presently receiving?

5. The access to information by organized and well financed criminals and terrorists make our citizens and country vulnerable to people who use our very laws against us.

(2) <u>Access to information through computer technology and the Internet</u>

When we add computer technology to the mix and our ability to access information electronically, it gives too many unscrupulous people the ability to assume almost anyone's identity. The boom in computer technology, the Internet and e-commerce has created limitless opportunities for fraud. The Internet provides opportunity for not just the traditional con games and schemes but new and innovative ways to defraud innocent people. Again, it's a perfect medium for thieves to remain anonymous.

Because the Internet offers virtual anonymity with no state or national boundaries, law enforcement and government agencies are forced into developing more creative and cooperative ways of combating Internet fraud. Unfortunately, it may be a case of too little too late. In the mid1990's, a special task force reported on the threat that terrorist activities relating to various types of computer technology and information system warfare would have on our citizens and our country. Back in 1996, the task force admitted we were behind in our defense strategies. They suggested combating the threat by consistently analyzing, updating and properly defending our in-place systems. They emphasized that not recognizing and dealing with the very real potential of information system terrorism could have extreme consequences.

In a separate effort to stimulate cooperative information sharing between government and law enforcement agencies in recognizing crime trends and organized fraud rings relating to Internet and identity fraud, the Federal Trade Commission created Consumer Sentinel. Consumer Sentinel is a database that provides information on broad trends and the volume of complaints prompted by particular Internet and identity theft schemes. When victims call the Federal Trade Commission to report identity theft they give their information to the Commission's department called Identity Theft Data Clearinghouse, which in turn, make the information available over the Internet to law enforcement agencies by way of their *Consumer Sentinel*. The Secret Service has placed agents in the FTC's Identity Theft Data Clearinghouse to better disseminate certain information and to develop and refer case leads in the hope of investigating more identity theft cases. Through the analysis of complaints and information in the Consumer Sentinel database, it is reported that the ten most frequently conducted scams on the Internet are:

- Internet Auction Fraud
- Internet Service Provider (ISP) Scams
- Internet Website Design/Promotions
- Internet Information and Adult Services (unauthorized credit card charges)
- Pyramid Scams
- Business Opportunities and Work-At-Home Scams

- Investment Schemes and Get-Rich-Quick Scams
- Travel/Vacation Fraud
- Telephone/Pay-Per-Call Solicitation Frauds
- Health Care Frauds

Cases involving identity theft on the Internet vary greatly. The FTC reported on an owner of a website it alleges offered fake ID templates over the Internet. The website advertised 45 day access to fake ID templates for $29.99. The site contained high quality templates to use in CREATING fake driver licenses from ten states. It also offered a birth certificate template, programs to generate bar codes required in some states to authenticate driver licenses and a program to falsify Social Security numbers.

Another scheme on the Internet involves "information brokers." Information brokers advertise on various websites that they can obtain consumer financial information. Many information brokers obtain your bank account balance by simply calling your bank to verify checking account information or by pretending they are you.

Because information is so easily accessed through the computer, it is very important when purchasing items, to determine if the Internet site you are purchasing from is encrypting your information. Don't just assume that they are. Sensitive personal information is too often stored on databases that can be accessed through poorly protected websites. Various Internet merchants have had customer's information such as their names, phone numbers, credit card numbers, bank names, account numbers and routing numbers stolen from their databases because the Internet merchants stored their customer's information in *plain text*! Hackers were able to easily download and sell this information. Even sites promising encryption and the latest in safeguards are having both internal problems and problems with outside hackers obtaining their database of customer information. According to information supplied in an article by the Privacy Times, a well-known

Internet bookseller fielded many customer complaints concerning customers' credit or debit cards being used to make additional purchases through fraudulent accounts set up using the unsuspecting customers' information.

Identity thieves' ability to purchase products from numerous on-line merchants dramatically increases the potential harm to consumers. These thieves can make an infinite amount of purchases with your credit information in relatively short periods of time. In addition, the dramatic growth of financial services such as mortgages, credit cards, bank accounts, credit reports and loans offered *on-line* provide both access to your information while offering anonymity to thieves.

Annually the IRS requests Americans file their tax returns electronically. It is supposed to make the review process for government workers easier and faster. This is not necessarily better and safer for the taxpayer but easier and faster for the reviewer. The Los Angeles Times reported that a member of the Senate Finance Committee asked the General Accounting Office to investigate the safety of *on-line filing* of your yearly IRS forms. I found the findings scary. It seems taxpayer's electronically filed returns are sometimes transmitted by computer to one of several **private companies** chosen by the IRS for review. These returns are eventually sent on to the agency for final filing. While investigating the security of the IRS electronic filing process, the General Accounting Office reportedly found many areas for concern. Some of their concerns involved the following:

➢ the security of the IRS electronic filing system was weak and outside access was accomplished easily.
➢ the agency needed tighter restrictions on its employees access to data
➢ proper safeguards were not in place by the private companies to guarantee that the very people viewing your return did not have criminal records
➢ many of the computer systems used by the private companies were not guaranteed secure.

Congress would eventually like tax returns filed electronically and has an established time frame for accomplishing this however, last year a little more than 25% of Americans filed this way. In light of recent GAO findings, it seems we Americans are not so foolish.

(3) Changes in the Uniform Commercial Code (UCC)

The Uniform Commercial Code, which has been substantially adopted as law in nearly every state, governs numerous areas of commercial law. State law supplemented by some federal law governs the operation of *checking accounts*. Article 4 of the Uniform Commercial Code, Bank Deposits And Collections, has been adopted at least in part in every state. It "defines rights between parties with respect to bank deposits and collections." The states, not the Federal government, are the primary source of law on commercial transactions in the U.S.

Changes in the Uniform Commercial Code shifted the responsibility of forged checks from the banks, onto the bank's account holders. The law now stresses *due diligence* and *comparative negligence*. The bank and the account holder split check fraud liability and monetary losses based upon the respective levels of fault. The Uniform Commercial Code clarifies an account holder's responsibility and the notification deadlines to alert the bank to suspected fraud. Account holders could be held liable if they are late in detecting the fraud. However, no matter who is determined responsible in individual cases of check fraud, we ultimately all carry the financial burden. The legal fees, exorbitant insurance rates and numerous additional bank costs related to this crime are ultimately passed on to guess who? Right, the consumer!

Do you remember the days you complained that banks held on to your check too long before making the funds available to you? Do you remember the phrase, "Be careful what you ask for, you might get it" or "every action has a reaction?" Under pressure from depositors, the Commercial Code laws were changed to accelerate check deposit availability. Banks are presently required to make funds available within two days for local checks and five days for out-of-town checks. These recent regulations have often forced banks to make funds available for check writing BEFORE previous deposits have actually cleared. This is a perfect scenario for check fraud.

One type of check fraud that takes advantage of this is called Check Kiting. Here's an example:

Your checks are stolen. You close the account. The criminals deposit some of your stolen, closed account checks (checks representing "0" funds) into a new account at a different bank through the bank's ATM. The float time between the ATM deposit and the checks drawn on the closed account reaching the issuing bank for payment can allow the criminals time to withdraw money (that does not exist) from the new account.

The scam works because deposited funds are made available to customers within days but financial institutions might not learn if a check is fraudulent for weeks.

(4) <u>Easy Access To Health Care Information</u>

I mentioned in the first chapter that dishonest employees having access to company information or databases could obtain your sensitive, nonpublic personal information contained in medical records or files. Investigators discovered that a female employed at a well-known children's hospital obtained the social security numbers of people from around the country that supplied requested medical information while participating in a national study. The collected social security numbers were eventually used to create false birth certificates, fraudulent social security cards and stolen identities. The impostors in turn, used the false identification to obtain instant credit for big screen televisions, computers and furniture.

There are numerous documented cases of physicians' and pharmacies' computer databases being comprised. Easy access to patient medical records is a well-known fact. The private practices of many doctors, dentists and other medical offices have little or no security or encryption software on their computers. We read many stories about health facilities not properly disposing of medical records. The careless disregard for the potential harm caused by this sensitive information falling into the wrong hands is unconscionable! We should demand more liability with accountability of the people and organizations entrusted with information that is required before services are rendered. The U.S. Department of Health and Human Services promises to help improve health privacy protection for consumers. They can be reached at www.hhs.gov or you can contact the Health Privacy Project, Institute for Health Care Research and Policy, Georgetown University Medical Center, 2233 Wisconsin Avenue, NW, Suite 525, Washington, DC 20007, 202-687-0880 www.healthprivacy.org.

(5) The Federal Financial Services Act a/k/a The Gramm-Leach- Bliley Act (and to many of my client's it's known as the OPT-OUT Act).

I am not going to get into all the provisions of this recent act but it is my opinion that this is another example of big business directly influencing Congress at the expense of the American consumer. This act created monumental changes in the financial service industries' regulation by eliminating the barriers between banking, insurance and investment services. Formerly separate and quite distinct financial institutions such as banks, insurance companies, brokerage services, credit unions, etc. were prohibited from merging. Banks for instance, were not allowed to own investment or brokerage firms. Brokerage firms were not allowed to sell insurance, etc. Each one service had its own regulatory agency. With the passing of this act and its deregulation of these financial service barriers came the financial service companies' ability to share their customer information among and between their *affiliated* companies! The financial service industry touted this as the best in service for consumers because they could offer a multitude of consumer financial services with a minimum of consumer inconvenience. (They also pushed its cost saving statistics). Realizing that this deregulation could create *some* consumer privacy problems and concerns, Congress decided it had better create some new responsibilities and rights concerning consumer financial privacy within the provisions of the act.

Under this act, the financial services industry's affiliations can now consist of banks, insurance companies and securities firms providing a "super store of services" to their customers. The government no longer regulates each type of financial service separately. Many people believe under the protection of this act that allows banks, credit unions, insurance and investment companies to be "affiliated companies," that our personally identifiable information is more available to more people and more businesses than ever before! This act not only allows these businesses to be affiliated with one another but also allows each of them to share your information with one another, without your *actual* consent! With the passing of this act is the ability for our personal information to be merged into shared databases without prior approval.

Congress' decision was to have provisions that required the financial service businesses to (1) at the least, disclose their *policies* regarding the sharing of consumers' personal financial information; (2) prohibit the disclosure of personally identifiable information to *unaffiliated* third parties, <u>unless the consumer is provided the right to **opt-out**.</u> Read this last sentence again. (If they *provide* you with the *opportunity* to opt-out, they may provide your personally identifiable information to *unaffiliated* third parties. Not **if** you opt-out, but if they provided you with the means to opt-out and you didn't opt-out. Get it? (3) Lastly, they require that the financial service companies have *in-place* security measures to protect consumers' nonpublic personal information. (Everyone has read about security breaches and you will read about more in this book so, guess how well that will work!)

Nonpublic personal information is information that has been made available to the company through its relationship with the consumer and has not been made available to the public or the "public at large". Some examples are medical records, insurance information, account numbers, access numbers, social security numbers, and other *confidential* information. *You* most often provide the personally identifiable and nonpublic information that is obtained by the financial institutions. It may be provided by way of a transaction with you or perhaps the information is obtained by providing a service to you.

Banks, insurance companies and securities firms may share your *nonpublic* personal information with "*affiliated* THIRD parties." They may also share your personal information with various joint venturers as long as they are "affiliated third parties." Key word here folks is *affiliated*. (Affiliated means various relationships between and among companies that are under common control with another company). Remember, unless you actually take the time to opt-out, they can also share your personal information with *unaffiliated* third parties, as long as they sent you a privacy notice with the opt-out provision.

Opt-out means that you must take action to keep your name or personal information from being used by certain companies and under certain conditions. Each year you must be given notice explaining your opt-out rights as they pertain to third party sharing. Typically the information is written on a small privacy policy notice and mailed out at least once per year along with your monthly statement. These notices are all too frequently overlooked. (One of the few companies that mails out a letter size privacy notice, in a separate mailing to its customers is State Farm Insurance. I am sure there are other companies that may do this but unfortunately most seem to slip them in with a monthly bill or statement). If you fail to perform the opt-out action, (if you take no action), it is interpreted as having given your consent to share your personal information with unaffiliated third parties! It differs from opt-in because, the "opt-in action" usually will not take place until you overtly give your consent. (This is a much better option for the consumer but not a better option for business). Business with the backing of Congress has succeeded in confusing consumers on the "opt-out" issue by allowing the consumer's information to be "in" unless they take the time to opt-out. Again, do you think this confusing and backward system is good for the average American consumer or big business? What these companies and businesses are counting on is your actually having to make the effort to deny them the right to share your information with unaffiliated third parties by making you physically have to opt-out. Businesses actually count on the tremendous amount of consumers that either don't understand "opting-out" or don't have the time to make the effort to opt-out. Make the effort. Try to control as much of your personal information as you've been given the opportunity to control. Financial institutions must disclose their privacy policies to you at the beginning of your relationship with them and then again once per year however, you don't have to opt-out each year. Your opt-out request should remain in- force until your relationship with that company changes or is severed.

Presently, there is little protection to defend against so many companies having access to your sensitive personal information. Although you may have given your sensitive and personal information to say your broker, with third party sharing, your nonpublic personal information can be given to a bank you do not actually bank with or an insurance company with which you have no direct relationship. This is information you did not directly give to them. It's a bit shocking and disconcerting to find out that a company you've never heard of...has your personal information. All of a sudden instead of the bank down the street having some of your private and personal information, many of the bank's affiliated partners across the country have it too! And how well can all these businesses guarantee protected access by others to your private information? As I've previously mentioned, to date many have not done very well. I am afraid we will see and hear about many more identity theft cases next year.

You now understand better your option to **"Opt-Out,"** or ask that your personal information not be shared with **_unaffiliated_** third parties. This may appear a dumb question but why would a company want to share their customer information with an unaffiliated third party? I don't get it. Are we opting-out of them sharing our personal information with businesses they did not intend to **share** our information with anyway? If that's the case, by opting-out, who are we really preventing from having our information? Or are they **selling** our information to unaffiliated companies if we don't opt-out? That could be a very lucrative profit center for many businesses. Or do they receive a percentage of the revenue that comes from "sharing" the personal information with the *unaffiliated third party*? Whatever they're doing, I want to prevent as many people from having access to my personal information as possible therefore, I opt-out. If I don't, who knows what information will be "*shared*" with whomever the financial service companies feel like sharing it, for whatever reason. It appears Congress picked big business over the best interest of the American public on much of this one. What do you think?

**(Financial institutions are prohibited from disclosing *account number information* to telemarketing, direct mail marketing or any other forms of electronic marketing).

**You may also Opt-Out of receiving unsolicited credit card offers by phoning 888-5-OPT-OUT. All three major credit bureaus use this number.

(6) Dishonest Employees

I illustrated earlier that there are dishonest employees that have access to your personal information. Information that can hurt you when it falls into the wrong hands.

The Associated Press reported on workers at an IRS processing center run by a large bank that actually hid approximately 40,000 tax returns or put them with papers to be shredded because they were behind in their work and apparently thought they would just dispose of the records. These workers showed very little regard for the consequences of their actions on the average taxpayer. It also illustrates the failure to place adequate safeguards to protect against such abuse of our personal information. Our tax returns not only contain private information we like to keep confidential but sensitive information such as social security numbers, our address, spouse's name, number of deductions, our occupations, and more. Having access to this information is like one stop shopping for identity theft.

In 1985, it was reported that the IRS discovered tax returns turning up in trash cans at the women's restroom of the agency's Philadelphia Service Center. Officials are said to have blamed the problem on costly computer problems and worker turnover at the center.

The LA Times reported a 1993 General Accounting Office study found that the FBI didn't keep track of potential misuse of its database. The GAO, an investigative arm of Congress, found a lack of personal passwords for people using the FBI's computer terminals. They reported that computer personnel were selling information to private detectives and helping criminals.

In another case, federal agents arrested and charged private investigators and social security employees with buying and selling confidential information from government computers.

After reading this chapter, you can no longer wonder how personal information gets into the hands of dishonest, unscrupulous, people. Now let us learn what happens after it's been in their hands.

Chapter 4

Identity Theft Agony: Trauma I & II

One of the saddest aspects of identity theft is that too often it's victims find themselves victimized twice, once by the impostor and then by the present system. Shortly after learning you were victimized, you most likely followed the initial suggestions offered by various organizations and authorities. Yet as the incidents of your fraud escalated, you discovered the information was too general and non-specific. Most guidance, suggestions and important information address the initial steps you should take once you discover you have been a victim of identity fraud. Advice and guidance are frequently printed in newspapers and magazine articles and typically cover the five initial steps everyone should take upon learning that they are a victim of this insidious crime. Let's review the important initial advice:

1. Report your theft to law enforcement. Get the officer or detective's information and phone number along with a copy of the police report and case number.

2. Contact all creditors and cancel all compromised accounts and credit cards. Follow-up all telephone conversations in writing.

3. Contact the fraud divisions of the three national credit reporting agencies, Experian, Equifax and Trans Union and place security and fraud alerts on your credit files and receive copies of your credit reports. Review your credit reports carefully and notify each agency of any incorrect or inaccurate information. Follow up in writing.

4. According to your particular circumstances, notify your bank, individual agencies such as the DMV, the Social Security Administration and the U.S. Postal Service.

5. Contact the Federal Trade Commission's hotline and visit their website.

You followed and completed most of the above list and thought you were finished? You thought it was over? You believed the crime was behind you and you could move on? Well, you're not alone. You, along with most identity theft victims, believe "it's over" after following the suggestions above, after placing the fraud alert and after making the necessary notifications. You followed all the suggestions and advice and more importantly, you did it in a timely fashion. You not only closed the compromised accounts, you have already received replacement credit cards. You even opened a post office box instead of having your new credit cards delivered to an unattended home mailbox. You wasted no time in placing special security features on bank and credit card accounts and received your credit reports within two weeks of the incident! You're finished, right? Well, perhaps you've completed what I, and my clients call "Trauma 1," more formally referred to as **Victimization Part I**. Welcome to **Victimization Part II!**

After having completed all the above, you quickly learn, "it ain't over." You need a lot more than the suggestions offered on websites and in newspaper articles. You need *real* answers for your *specific* circumstances. You need to understand why it's not going away! You quickly become overwhelmed. What all the websites, newspapers and magazine articles failed to explain to you is that under the present system, identity theft victims must continually prove their innocence regarding fraudulent claims, acts and activity performed in their name. Discovering yourself burdened with debts you did not authorize and creditors that don't believe you, you simply don't know how to proceed. My friend, this is "trauma 2-the present system," more formally known as **Victimization Part II.**

Under the present system, you've tried to put the brakes on further activity by making other people, agencies and authorities aware of what has happened to you. Even so, the burden has still fallen on you to <u>prove</u> that you are, in fact, *a victim.* You still have to prove it's not you running up your accounts or opening new accounts. To help prove you are truly a victim of fraud, it's important to obtain a police report and case number. However, obtaining a police report could prove difficult. In most states, the way the law is presently written, the victim needs to report the identity theft incident to law enforcement *in the jurisdiction in which the theft occurred.* (I am not referring to fraud over the Internet). Many, many victims have no idea where the theft occurred. Identity thieves often move from state to state or can in fact, operate from a completely different COUNTRY while performing these illegal acts. Moreover, many local police departments have one officer or detective assigned many duties. Many find they don't have the time or ability to pursue cases with low apprehension and conviction rates. So, for several reasons, a police report may not be written and a case number not issued making your burden of proof even more difficult, complicated and time consuming.

Although you closed your hijacked credit card accounts and you may only be financially libel for up to fifty dollars to the credit card company, the merchants and collection agencies might have reported your delinquent accounts to the three national credit reporting agencies. And if your checkbook was stolen, all the merchants that unknowingly accepted your fraudulent checks still want their money. As far as the merchants are concerned, you wrote those bad checks. So, every time the thief writes a check and that merchant is not paid, expect strong letters from the merchant and then threatening letters from their collection agency. If credit cards continue to be fraudulently applied for, granted and used, the creditors will hound you about bills you're not paying. Until you are aware of these accounts, your credit reports will reflect the (unauthorized) activity along with any delinquent payments, reported by the very creditors that extended the unauthorized credit!

The only way to try to vindicate yourself is to answer every merchant, creditor and collection agency that notifies you of an outstanding or delinquent debt. Of course, notification from them typically is stern and demanding and depending on the number of letters they have sent you, might even be threatening. You find yourself constantly placed in a defensive position. The (fraudulent) activity has already taken place. After notifying each merchant and creditor of your incident, they inform you that they want *proof* that you are truly a victim of fraud. They may want you to complete and have notarized their "specific" forgery affidavit as further evidence of your innocence. An affidavit of forgery is a document containing information you provide on the fraudulent activity along with your notarized signature certifying the information you provided is true and correct under penalty of the law. Each forgery affidavit refers to specific information about the fraud perpetrated against you. It will typically ask you to complete the date you became aware of the fraud, the fraudulent or compromised account numbers, a police case number and any other information that is pertinent to the crime.

After completing and mailing all of these affidavits, you still might receive letters of demand from the collection agencies representing the creditors and merchants. It seems the collection agencies and their clients don't talk as often as they should. You inform the creditors that you are still receiving collection letters. They say they are working on it. You end up mailing the collection agency the same information and documentation you sent the creditors and merchants. Many times the collection agencies won't even acknowledge receipt of your documentation. Why? Frequently, it's because their collection letters are generated by computers that did not receive the payment or M-O-N-E-Y. So, the collection agency that received your documents instead of M-O-N-E-Y, will most likely generate and mail you another letter requesting payment. The collection agency might mail you numerous collection letters and while you persevere in your attempts to contact them and their contractor, the thief continues perpetrating the crime. More documentation, more affidavits, more time, more frustration. Additionally, every phone call you make notifying various creditors must be documented. You must be organized. You must keep names, dates, companies and times of each phone call. Most victims are not able to be as organized as they need to be. Not keeping good notes or a log of dates, phone numbers, names, companies you have notified, and various instructions and comments, further complicates your situation and delays the process. This is the saga of identity theft. No one really explains **Victimization Part II** so don't feel bad that you didn't expect it.

Further complicating your victimization and after following everyone's advice to place a fraud-security alert on your credit file, your impostor opens yet another account. A cellular phone account is opened using your social security number under the "absolutely no credit verification" offer made by numerous wireless phone companies. The thief immediately runs up exorbitant and soon to be delinquent bills. The fraud alert or victim's statement you placed with the credit reporting agencies didn't even come into play here. This creditor made no attempt to verify that it was actually you requesting service. However, the creditor *is* looking to you for payment of the account!

This scenario is not an exaggeration and it is not atypical. Very often, as with many of my clients, you are unaware that the thief has taken out a car loan, rented an apartment or opened a wireless service account until someone comes along seeking payment or you are denied a loan because your credit report is no longer glowing but in fact, full of bad debt and unauthorized activity. An excellent credit history that may have taken you a lifetime to establish is...history. You can become overwhelmed, angry and frustrated over creditor's confusion and disbelief as to who really ran up the bills. You are in a perpetual state of proving it's not you. The money, time and effort are exhausting. The amount of calls and notices you receive can be both traumatic and scary. The amount of documentation you must provide can be exhausting. It takes time and a tremendous amount of effort to notify all agencies, complete fraud reports, contact creditors, confirm the contact, provide the correct documentation, have each creditor's affidavit notarized, follow up on the creditor's corrections to the credit bureaus, verify your file's deletions or corrections, contact the credit bureaus and complete *their* correction forms, mail duplicates of your supporting documentation, and so on. Proving unauthorized and erroneous accounts and information on your credit reports, asking each to investigate and make the necessary corrections and trying to regain your identity and credit standing can sometimes take years. In addition to all this, you still have your life, your career, and your family. Identity fraud takes its toll on you emotionally, physically, psychologically and financially. The most common complaint I receive when I first meet my clients is the fear that it will never end and that it might even get worse! Losing a solid credit history that took you a lifetime to build and the constant worrying about acts your impostor might be perpetrating is at the least, unsettling and at the most traumatizing.

Having your identity violated is awful but when the majority of authorities don't believe you, it's a nightmare. Knowing that most victims usually don't know where to begin, how to proceed or even why they can't just ignore the bad credit, collection notices or inaccurate credit reports is the reason behind both this book and my consulting company, Identity Theft Management. I know that recovery from identity theft is difficult. I know that the only way identity theft victims can hope to regain some control over their personal information and try to recover from being victimized is to "manage the theft." I know victims need more than generic suggestions and tips to help them navigate through the often lengthy and time consuming ordeal. But most of all, I know that most victims need *individual* guidance, direction and support along with help, information and realistic expectations to demystify a confusing and frustrating crime.

One of my clients followed all the steps mentioned above. After having made all his notifications, having supplied all the documentation everyone demanded, his utility company actually gave an impostor electric power under his account! Using my client's name, the thief simply telephoned the utility company and requested power. Once my client discovered the fraud he asked the utility company why they simply extended credit over the phone without proper verification. They replied that my client's history had always been so good with them that they didn't see a problem extending him additional utilities upon request. Unfortunately, my client was not the one that got the power!

Well, it's been three months since you last received your credit reports so you've decide to request and review them again. They arrive and you immediately see activity that you have already notified the credit reporting agencies was fraudulent. Additionally, an incorrect account that they had previously deleted has somehow reappeared! This is the *pinnacle* of the identity theft trauma. Occasionally after contacting the creditor for investigation, the creditor determines that the accounts opened by the impostor are *accurate* and they refuse to tell the credit reporting agency to change or delete the information. This could happen when the creditor, i.e. ABC department store, verifies that the fraudulent purchases are in fact, yours and they refuse to send the credit reporting agency, (credit bureau), information to the contrary. It can also happen when one credit reporting agency removes the inaccurate information yet the corrections are not made by the other agencies. It can happen for a host of reasons but in the end, you again have another ineffective component of the system with which to contend. The amendments made to the Fair Credit Reporting Act back in 1997 were supposed to address some of these very issues and they have...to a point. One of the biggest contentions was corrected by changing the burden of proof *from the consumer* on to the credit bureaus when the consumer questions inaccurate or erroneous information appearing on their report. If the creditor cannot support the information, the credit reporting agency must correct or delete the information in accordance with the consumer's request. This change was a milestone for consumer rights with respect to their credit reports however; from an identity theft victim's view point, the tediousness of working with the creditors and the credit reporting agencies has not changed much. Typically, ID theft victims have numerous unauthorized activity appearing on their credit reports, not just one or two accounts. Notifying the creditors of the unauthorized accounts; the documentation required in order to prove account fraud to each of the creditors; following up that the creditors in turn, notify the credit reporting agencies and then having to supply each of the credit reporting agencies with the supporting documentation when the creditor neglects to contact them; waiting for the credit reporting agency to verify your documentation with the creditor and then hopefully, having your report corrected...is still a nightmare.

The daily and unsolicited credit card offers that stuff our mailboxes along with the "instant credit" jingles that permeate television and radio advertisements also add to our vulnerability. Frequently, little or no actual verification is done to ensure that the person requesting credit is actually the person they say they are. However, when things go wrong, the creditors, who so greedily accepted fraudulent credit applications and gave instant unverified credit, claim to be as much a victim as the person they helped victimize! They are also the ones demanding *you prove* that it "was not you" who asked for the credit. Instead of your having to prove it was not you, why didn't they prove it WAS you before extending the credit? Creditors have gotten away with this activity for years at the expense of the consumer. They assume the risk of making lots of money, while you assume the risk of them offering "easy credit" to the wrong person. Their credit history is not destroyed when something goes wrong. They don't have to go through the mess of proving their innocence. They often don't really have to pay for the losses either. They pass much of that on to you too. So, where's their incentive to stop? Well, the incentive should come from Congress. It should come from consumer agencies like the FTC. It should come from consumer advocates that are supposed to look out for us. It should come from the consumer. Now that you are aware of the catch-22 of this problem, it should certainly come from you. We should demand that this practice stop. When creditors continue to get away with this type of activity, it adds to your recovery time. When creditors choose to disregard fraud alerts or victims statements, on your credit reports, it adds to your recovery time. When creditors choose not to verify identification, it adds to your vulnerability and recovery time. When the present system is overrun with this type of crime and no one addresses the problems of the S-Y-S-T-E-M, it adds both time and trauma to your victimization.

Furthering the recovery period is the fact that financial institutions, financial service companies and most businesses have insurance to cover their losses so their incentive to litigate your type of identity fraud case may be absent. They have little to no interest in litigating small identity theft cases. They are aware that their chances of getting any restitution are slim. Even after some identity thieves are identified and arrested, many prosecutors are either not interested or have a strong incentive to work a plea bargain because individual identity theft cases can be expensive and time consuming to prosecute. They also know many judges don't give jail time to nonviolent criminals, especially if the defendant is a first-time offender. And guess who else knows? Right, the criminal.

Chapter 5

Being Victimized Changes You

Going through all of this will change you. Being victimized changes you. How can it not change you? You become much more aware. You become much more private. You become more suspicious. Sometimes more cynical, definitely more guarded, less trusting and almost but not quite contemptuous. Being victimized by your identity thief changes you. The crime's effects are insidious. You may not realize the changes right away. At first, you believed you were only fighting the bad guys, the thieves, your impostors. Eventually you realize you are fighting on a number of different fronts. You're not only fighting to stop the thieves' fraudulent activities. You are fighting to get the creditors to stop issuing credit to impostors under your social security number. You are fighting to clear your name and prove your innocence. You are fighting to correct a ruined credit history. You are fighting to get the required supporting documentation you need. You are fighting to have credit grantors and credit bureaus acknowledge your documentation and make the appropriate corrections. You are fighting to keep the bogus information from arbitrarily returning. You are fighting a system. Believe me, you are never the same person you were before this happened to you. This crime changes you. After prolonged frustration, anger, disappointment, resentment, confusion and a host of other emotions, anyone would change. Once it has taken its toll, you definitely realize it. Being victimized changes you. I know it changes you because I work with victims of identity theft everyday. I go through the frustrating and traumatizing events of identity fraud everyday. I know it changes you. I know it changed me.

When it initially happened to me, I felt overwhelmed, angry and most of all frustrated! What had I done to cause the agony I was going through? Why had these impostors selected me? Why was I the lucky one? What made these criminals decide to live-it-up on *my* good name? I was overwhelmed by the amount of letters and threats I received from merchants, creditors and collection agencies. I was angry because these thieves were destroying an excellent credit history that took a lifetime to establish. I was frustrated because I wasn't certain about the best way to respond to all the letters and notices I was receiving. And I certainly didn't have the T-I-M-E to contact and re-contact every merchant and creditor while holding down a very full and demanding position. That was a job in itself!

During the first few months of my eighteen month ordeal, as I retrieved each day's mail full of creditor's letters and collection agency notices, my nerves made me so sick that my husband had to eventually take over collecting the mail. I stopped reading the mail at night because I would become so upset, I couldn't sleep. I learned never to read the mail on weekends because it destroyed whatever plans we'd made. After a while, I developed a routine where I only opened the dreaded notices and read mail in the morning, Monday through Friday. As I've previously mentioned, there is very little assistance for white-collar crimes like this. When I told people what happened to me and what I was going through, they had little sympathy. In fact, most had no idea what I was talking about. Even the police I reported my crime to were much more concerned with violent crimes and therefore offered little more than a sympathetic ear. (In 1997, when my identity theft occurred, Orlando's law enforcement was little equipped to handle crimes like identity theft. Today, their economic crimes division handles numerous cases of id theft. Still, many police departments in cities and towns across the nation offer little or no assistance to victims of this crime).

Up until this incident, I resolved problems by being assertive, persistent, and goal oriented. One day, seeing the state I was in, my father and former business partner asked me why I seemed to be taking a back seat to these thieves and allowing them to destroy what I had worked so hard to attain. He asked me why I viewed overcoming business obstacles differently than overcoming this personal obstacle. I told him it was probably due to my lack of objectivity. I explained that this problem was a *personal* attack. I felt lost. I felt alone. No one was willing to listening to me. I didn't know *who* was attacking me, *why* they chose me, and *where* and *when* they would attack next. I felt an overwhelming sense of dread and apprehension all the time. (To this day, I can't find a better word than just plain OVERWHELMED to describe the consistently heavy burden I carried around with me all the time). I was not objective. How could I be? This problem was happening to ME. Better said, this problem was someone else being ME. And my problems were not just with my identity thieves. The creditors and collection agencies didn't want to deal with me either. Nooooooo, to them I was guilty and had to prove my innocence. And when I tried to prove my innocence, they didn't want to hear my story. They wanted money. They wanted repayment of a debt. Until their computer-generated letters received MONEY, I was going to continue to receive letters. They also didn't want to acknowledge the responsibility of having accepted bad checks. They didn't want to acknowledge they had accepted checks with a fraudulent driver's license as identification. They didn't want to acknowledge that they accepted a fraudulent credit card. No, at the time of the transactions they were too busy being deliriously happy at the huge sales they were making. I unloaded all of this on my dad. He simply replied, "It sounds to me as if you're falling back on emotions instead of relying on your business acumen." (For ten years, I was Chief Operating Officer of a successful real estate and development company). I'm sure that I sounded emotional. I *was* emotional. It was a very emotional situation. I replied, "No one is helping me. The police aren't helping me. The creditors aren't listening to me. No one really believes me. No one even understands what I'm going through. I don't know the enemy. I don't know what they are going to do next. I don't know who is going to come after me for fraudulent accounts and debts tomorrow. I don't know when it's going to stop and on top of all this I'm receiving threatening letters from companies telling me that I could go to jail!" My words hung in the air as we both sat facing each other. Finally, my father said, "Sounds like you need a good business plan. You know what your goal is. It's to regain your identity. Now what are the objectives for reaching your goal?" Could I really be that detached? Could I view the total destruction of my life's credit history as just another obstacle that must be overcome? I could hear my father's answer without having asked the question. Do you have a choice?

Well, I got organized. I prioritized. I was proactive. I devised a plan. I created systems. The more detached I was, the more effective I became. I worked ON the problem instead of waiting for the thieves' next move and defending myself against their actions. I was practical. I became determined not to allow the thieves to destroy even more important things than my credit history. They could not take the qualities I liked best in myself. I was a successful business woman who started to react like a frightened turtle. I wanted to crawl inside my shell and have it all just go away. Determination and persistence had always brought me success. I became determined to stop the constant threats and harassment by merchants, creditors and collection agencies when I had the proper documentation to prove my victim status. I persisted in trying to stop creditors from extending even more fraudulent credit in my name. I was back! My work ethic kicked in. I was persistent. I was hard working. I was thorough and I was goal oriented. Every demand notice I received, got a response. Each notification I sent was concise but contained all the required supporting documentation to prove I had been a crime victim. When they sent a second, third and fourth letter, I responded a second, third and fourth time. Always documenting the previous correspondence. When it was time to respond to a higher official within a company, they were contacted. When a branch of a large corporation was defrauded in my name, I proactively mailed the corporate headquarters the information on the fraudulent activity as well, thereby putting them on notice of possible future fraudulent activity. It wasn't easy. It was tremendously time consuming. It was frustrating. It was my second job. But, I got my identity back! And in the world we live in today, with the ease in which personal information is available, it is a daily struggle to keep!

As a result of my success, I had countless requests from other victims for assistance. My company, Identity Theft Management™ and this book were created out of their need. Five years after my victimization, I still get apprehensive when collecting my mail. I still look through the stack of bills and letters convinced that my ordeal will begin all over again and that I will find creditor or collection letters threatening my present status. And there are other remnants and signs of having been victimized.

> ➢ I shred or tear into pieces every scrap of paper with any personally identifiable information on it such as my name, address, account number.

> ➢ I am not a person who enjoys confrontation however; I have absolutely no problem challenging anyone who wants my personal information when I don't see a reason or benefit of them having it.

> ➢ I do not complete warranty cards requiring any personal information, ever! I figure, if the item breaks during the warranty period, I will raise such an uproar that the store will replace the item so they do not have to deal with me.

> ➢ I never talk with anyone taking a survey over the phone. I don't speak with telemarketers, people taking news show polls, political polls, or marketing surveys.

➢ I never have my personal checks delivered to my home mailbox. I have them delivered to my bank's main location and personally pick them up.

➢ My checks do not have my home address or phone number preprinted on them.

➢ I do not place outgoing bills with checks in my home mailbox.

➢ I never leave my purse or wallet in an unattended car.

➢ I never place my purse in the child's seat of a cart while I shop. And I am always conscious of having my purse closed or zippered.

➢ Galleries, stores or websites that ask me to sign their guest books so that they can make me aware of upcoming events, specials or sales, never get my name, address or phone number.

➢ Mail-in offers asking me to complete my name and address so they can mail additional savings and coupons, get tossed with the other trash.

➢ Free merchandise offers that require any personal information go unclaimed.

➢ All my personal phone numbers are unpublished and unlisted.

➢ I never voluntarily give my personal e-mail address to people or entities I don't know. I try hard not to invite viruses, spam and hackers.

➢ I never register any personal information with a website in order to view the website. There are far too many sites available that do not require my information.

➢ Once I found out my college's annual biographical update was sold to various businesses for marketing purposes, I never completed another update request card from them.

➢ I never complete store guest books or store contests or drawings. It is just another way to obtain your personal information.

➢ I mail Opt-Out forms to every financial institution I deal with. This includes my banks, credit card companies, investment brokers, insurance companies, and credit reporting agencies. (Although with the passing of the Federal Financial Modernization Act, Opting-Out doesn't restrict much information anymore).

➢ I don't draw attention to myself by having cute, personal license tags on my cars that might cause anyone to look up the owner. (This, by the way, is quite simple to do).

➢ I try to use my post office box address and not my personal residence address when completing address requests.

➢ I try not to fax documents containing *any* sensitive personal information. I never fax copies of checks with my account and routing number. I had faxed documents go astray, been lost, faxed to the wrong number or received by someone who did not give it to the intended party. In the past, I have actually *received* faxed documents meant for another company that contained highly confidential information. Always be aware that when you fax documents, you never really know who might be viewing them.

➢ To provide my social security number is like getting milk from a stone. I even find it difficult to give it to my doctor's office personnel.

➢ I have not refinanced my home in 15 years because I do not want all my information traveling over the Internet on its way to Fannie Mae.

➢ I try to keep all personal information off the hard drive of my computer.

➢ I limit the amount of personal information I send in e-mails.

There are hundreds of other things I do or don't do as a direct consequence of having had my identity stolen. Being victimized changes you. It leaves its legacy.

Because it's hard to determine if or when it's over, many victims find themselves worrying about what "might be happening." What fraudulent activities "might they be doing" in my name? People that know and love you may comment about your *being paranoid*. Paranoia is the <u>delusion</u> of persecution. In reality, it was probably no delusion. You probably were being persecuted! Moreover, you may not know if or when the persecution has ended. Things might be fine for a while and you think it's ended but within six months you receive bills or collection notices and you know…it's not over. I know of victims who have not successfully addressed all the necessary issues and for them, their identity theft has gone on for years. Things can get progressively worse. It is a devastating crime with potentially traumatizing consequences. This crime leaves it's victims to contend with emotional, physical, psychological and financial effects. You aren't given a choice. Being victimized will change you.

Chapter 6

Things I Bet You Didn't Know

I bet you didn't know...

...that with all the attention focused on the prevalence of this crime many people still don't follow the warnings and safe guards suggested by the Federal Trade Commission, various Departments of Law Enforcement and other organizations such as mine, Identity Theft Management. However, the bigger problem is that you can be one of those informed consumers following the advice and suggestions offered by others and still become a victim of this devastating crime.

...that financial institutions and many businesses often have sufficient insurance to cover their losses due to fraud so when dealing with the smaller amounts in most cases of identity fraud the incentive to apprehend and prosecute is often absent.

...that identity theft is the fastest growing crime in America today but in some states, it's not labeled as a "crime." In order to prosecute the criminal that stole your personal information for their financial gain, many states charge the criminal with the federal law of "misuse of a social security number." (Arizona was the first state in the nation to make identity theft a felony).

...that the real numbers of identity theft cases in our country are hard to track. Identity theft cases are reported by numerous agencies including federal, state and local law enforcement, the FTC, the American Bankers Association and others.

...that it's very, very hard in today's world to protect access to your personal information. In order to obtain credit, in order to be seen by a doctor, you must give personal information and once that information is in the public domain, it's very difficult to protect.

...that it's more difficult to prove your official "victim status" without a police report and case number however, except for Internet fraud, most incidents of identity theft must be reported in the jurisdiction in which the crime took place. Many victims have no idea where the crime took place.

...that most police cannot possibly handle, let alone solve the staggering number of identity theft cases in addition to other forms of crime.

...that credit card companies issuing unrequested, pre-approved credit card offers in the mail often don't screen carefully enough for impostor applicants thus adding significantly to the growing number of victims.
...that federal law prohibits creditors from mailing you new credit cards you did not specifically request.

...that a checking account with over-draft protection are vulnerable to a check thief not only going through the money in your checking account but the money used in an additional account to cover overages.

...that victimized account holders could be held liable if late in detecting check or other bank fraud perpetrated against them. [*See Changes In The Uniform Commercial Code In Chapter 2*].

...that the majority of banks are better prepared to handle business fraud; that is fraud within the bank and against the bank, then they are fraud against their account holders.

…that it is a violation of some state's laws for a merchant to require a consumer to produce a credit card number for identification when paying by check however, a consumer can be required to show that they have a valid credit card. The merchant can then note the type of card such as Visa or Master Card, and the name of the issuing bank, but nothing else.

…that many people assume Social Security Numbers are unique. They were intended by the Social Security Administration to be unique, but the Social Security Administration didn't take sufficient precautions to ensure that they were. A previously issued number has been given to someone with the same name and birth date as the original recipient several times by the Social Security Administration, thinking it was the same person asking again.

…that the only legal way to get a new social security number is to talk to the Social Security Administration and they are very reluctant to issue a new number. You also must deal with them <u>directly</u> to legally obtain a new number. Companies or people that promise to get you a new number may not be legal and are unlikely to actually accomplish it.

…that according to a report issued by the Office of the Inspector General concerning abuses of social security numbers and its relationship with identity theft, senior citizens were not targeted for this type of abuse anymore than any other group.

…that the hotline's abuse allegation calls to the social security administration included many identity theft abuses as well as people complaining of their social security number having been assigned to other people.

…that in many states the names and addresses from the motor vehicle and driver license files are public record and may be provided to companies for use in marketing programs about product announcements, sales events, credit offers, and other advertising. And although you request that your personal information be withheld by completing the necessary forms and opt-out requests, your name and address may still be released for use in marketing programs.

…that many prosecutors have a strong incentive to work a plea deal with your identity thief because many judges aren't likely to give jail time to nonviolent criminals, especially if the dollar amount is relatively small or the defendant is a first-time offender.

…that many major corporations, schools and government agencies are finding alternatives to the Social Security Number as your form of identification.

…that under existing law, people convicted of identity theft and other white-collar crimes often receive light sentences in large part because the victims aren't *physically* injured.

…that when it happens to you, you find very few people listen and very few understand. In fact, *you* were one of those people…until you became a target, a victim.

…that it will take considerable time, money and effort to try and clear your name, correct your credit reports and get back your identity.

…that almost anything can be learned about anybody in the United States today. With the Freedom Of Information Act, the Internet and social security numbers used as employee identification, financial identification, medical identification and so on, we have destroyed our ability to keep certain information private therefore, in reality, "Privacy" in our country has become a concept, no longer a reality.

...that local police, various law enforcement agencies, secret service and Congress are overwhelmed as to how to handle the staggering numbers of identity theft victims.

...that the police, various law enforcement agencies, secret service, and Congress don't know how to handle the staggering number of perpetrators of these crimes.

...that financial service companies can share your personal information with affiliated companies without your overt consent. When your banker, insurer and investment broker are affiliated, your banker may have access to your insurance information, your broker may have access to your bank information and so on.

...that with health care information being stored and shared on computers, it is a good idea to be aware of who has your health information and how it is being used.

...that debt collectors cannot harass you or call you at work if you tell them that such calls are not permitted.

...that if you simply cut up your credit cards, the creditor is not aware that you destroyed them...the account is still open.

...that the Medical Information Bureau is a data bank used by insurance companies. You may obtain a copy of your file to make sure the information it contains is correct by writing to the MIB, PO Box 105, Essex Station, Boston, MA 02112. For more information log on to: www.hhs.gov

...that according to the Fair Credit Reporting Act, you may prohibit your name from appearing on credit reporting agencies lists for unsolicited credit and insurance offers. To exercise your right to be kept off the lists for two years you may telephone 1-888-567-8688 or complete and return the individual credit reporting agencies' form and you must be taken off the lists indefinitely. This is considered *Opting Out.*

...that when you send e-mails your mail goes from one server to another until the desired destination is reached. All along the way, any of the administrators of the servers have access to any information you include in your e-mail.

...that there are security inks that react with common chemicals should a forger try to modify or alter your check. Make sure your personal checks have some form of security feature.

...that one of the largest, best organized and well financed crime rings involved with the manufacture and use of fraudulent identification is the Nigerian crime ring living within the United States.

...that the largest number of identity theft complaints come from California, New York, Florida and Texas however, the largest number of complaints per 100,000 people are from, in order, District of Columbia, California, New York and Maryland.

Chapter 7

The Scary Part:
It's Out There and It's Waiting for You!

Let's discuss some of the characteristics of this crime. As its victim, you frequently have no idea who is impersonating you. You often don't know how your impersonators obtained your personal information. You're typically unaware of the crimes they're committing in your name until well after they commit them. You have little idea how long they will impersonate you or the extent of the damage they will impart. And once your identity is stolen, you will find limited help and assistance dealing with the consequences.

I often talk with people who know little about the effects of identity theft. I explain the destructive havoc this crime imposes on its victims. My audience habitually responds with sincerity and innocence and questions the extent of ruin when the maximum liability to the credit card companies for unauthorized debts is fifty dollars. At this point in the discussion, I feel weighed down. How do I begin to describe the succession of tasks that lay in front of many identity theft victims?

I begin by explaining that although many laws are on their side, the law is not going to help get their good name and credit back. I tell them they are going to have to work like crazy and even then, it might be a long time coming. I proceed to undermine their naive belief that fifty dollars per credit card is their entire financial risk. I explain that although federal law only allows creditors to hold consumers liable for up to fifty dollars of unauthorized debts per card, the effects of unauthorized charges, new credit card accounts and delinquencies on their credit reports is devastating. I explain that they might endure the consequences of the fraudulent activity for many years. Their eyebrows usually begin to inch upward. I continue. As an identity fraud victim, you will discover the amount of unauthorized loans, services and goods your thieves have received only after mysterious creditors call you with the bad news; you request your credit reports and view their criminal activity or after enduring a steady flow of creditor and collection agency telephone calls and notices demanding payment for debts they incurred in *your* name. The constant harassing phone calls and notices along with the hours of tedious documentation you will need to supply will take the place of the golf or family time you had before. You will no longer recognize your credit history as belonging to you. Just as the look of total disbelief comes over my audience, I remind them that without a glowing credit history, they could be denied employment, loans, credit cards, the refinancing they intended or that investment opportunity! You will wonder if it will ever stop. Your new hobby is "proving your innocence and victim status." You find yourself continuously trying to prove that is wasn't you or a family member that ran up the debt or opened the fraudulent accounts. Just as you convince one creditor of your victim status and clear one fraudulent account, another appears. It is a never-ending battle because unless you are proactive or the thieves are caught and convicted, the perpetrator has very little reason to stop. Somewhere around this point, they mumble, "Why didn't we know this? Why weren't we told?" I repeat, "Why weren't you told? Well, that's the scary part."

Identity theft comes in many colors and flavors, many sizes and shapes. Too many people think it is just about stolen wallets. What makes it so scary is that it is about a whole lot more.

The crime itself has become quite familiar. You go out to a restaurant, pay by credit card and then days later find charges to your credit card you did not make.

Here's an even scarier incident. A clerk hired as a temporary worker for one of the nation's largest credit bureaus, (which are now most often referred to as credit reporting agencies), allegedly downloaded the names, social security numbers, work histories and other personal facts from the credit agencies' database and led a ring of identity thieves. According to a report made by the credit reporting agency, the human resource company supplying the temporary worker failed to perform the required background check. The proliferation of corporate America's use of temporary and outsourced workers makes this a recurrent type of problem. Temporary workers that hold no loyalty to the company or the customer, yet have access to company databases can and do use personal and private information for illegal purposes and their own financial gain. Scary!

The fastest growing white-collar crime, the crime that claimed an estimated 750,000 victims in 1999 is a crime that is all too often put on the back burner. Individual cases of identity theft often get progressively worse before getting better. It's a crime that can stalk its victims for years. Why do we procrastinate when it comes to really dealing with this crime? There are a variety of answers to this question. Your local police are often busy with violent crime, so even when they would like to assist you, they cannot. In addition, numerous police departments across the country have a single detective assigned to handle the tremendous economic or financial crimes caseload. Police are spread very thin and know that getting these criminals convicted is extremely time consuming and difficult. Criminals convicted of identity theft and other white-collar offenses are typically given light sentences because victims are not physically hurt. (You can't physically SEE the emotional and psychological trauma many victims endure). The financial implications for the victim often start months *after* they have reported the crime and can get progressively worse as time goes on. Although the duty of the police department to its citizens is to find and apprehend perpetrators of crimes, identity theft is compounded by the fact that often victims don't know *who* committed the crime against them, *how* the theft occurred, *when* the theft occurred, *where* the theft took place and the extent of the damage. The acts of these thieves are often random and spread over a wide area covering numerous states or countries. When I was victimized, the detective working my case in Orange County, Florida said, "LouAnn, you weren't raped and you were killed. This is very low on my list of priorities." My identity theft was back in 1997 before Florida had established special units and task forces to handle crimes specifically associated with economic crimes of fraud and identity theft. In 1997, the detective assigned to my case was also working murder cases and was up front with me about the amount of assistance I could expect from him. None. The states leading the nation today in this type of fraud are California, New York, Florida and Texas. They are also the nation's leaders in enacting new laws, organizing special task forces and establishing specific economic crimes divisions within departments to handle crimes like identity theft.

However, in most of our cities and counties, the overwhelming number of incidents far out number the amount of law enforcement officers dedicated to investigating this type of crime. Additionally, in most states, in order for the police department to write up an incident report, the law states that the crime had to have happened in their jurisdiction. Well, again, most of the time victims don't know *who* did it, *when* they did it or *where* they did it! Many of my clients are initially denied police reports due to this law. When law enforcement is successful in apprehending an identity thief, most know a conviction is difficult. Both police and prosecutors know that individual, first time offenders are rarely convicted and if convicted, typically get a mere slap on the wrist. So, we victims are left waiting for identity thieves to commit second, third or fourth offenses or for them to join organized identity theft rings where their crimes are committed against groups of people and not just individuals, before our system and our laws kick in. Sad and Scary.

There is some good in having it so bad. Only when things get really, really bad and almost out of control, does our society realize action must be taken before utter chaos reigns supreme and control might be impossible. As a nation, we are nearing that point. Gradually our legislators on both the state and federal levels are recognizing the effects this crime has on victims and our society as a whole. New policies, bills and legislation are being created. For years, the victim of identity fraud not only suffered the effects of financial liability but also had to defend themselves against the collection methods of creditors and merchants. The "victim" was not the individual who had their identity stolen but the creditor or merchant that suffered the financial loss of goods or services. With the enactment of bills like The Identity Theft Assumption and Deterrence Act, (The Identity Theft Act), financial liability for unauthorized credit card purchases is often limited and *individuals* as well as creditors and merchants are *supposed* to be viewed as victims. Unfortunately, in reality, many victims find merchants, creditors, banks, and collection agencies treat them as guilty and they must PROVE their innocence and their victim status!

Under the Identity Theft Act, it is a federal crime for someone to knowingly transfer or use, without lawful authority, a means of identification of another person with the intent to commit, or to aid or abet, any unlawful activity that constitutes a violation of federal law, or that constitutes a felony under any applicable state or local law.

Under the Identity Theft Act, a name or social security number is considered a means of identification. A credit card number, cellular telephone electronic serial number or any other piece of information that may be used alone or in conjunction with other information to identify a specific individual is also considered a means of identification. Our government is enacting quite a few laws but the crime remains rampant and out of control. We have more laws to guard against this crime than at any other time in the history of the country yet the crime remains out-of-control. Obviously, laws alone are not working. Scary but true.

One of the scariest aspects of this crime is when you discover that someone has been impersonating you for years and you hadn't the slightest clue. Due to the illegal actions of their impostors, many victims find out they are wanted on various charges when they register to vote or apply for a driver license, or apply for a job requiring a background check or security clearance. It is a devastating and at times, life altering crime. Equally as problematic is the fact that victims are forced to react defensively when you learn an impostor is committing theft and fraud in your name. Knowing that an offensive position is always better, you assume you must be doing something wrong and seek the advice of various agencies that deal with identity theft, only to learn that their counsel can also have you operating *defensively*. The credit reporting agencies, the offices of Attorneys General, the Federal Trade Commission, law enforcement agencies and fraud advisors will tell you what to do and who to contact to cancel your cards and how to notify authorities of your victimization. They will explain how to guard and *defend* your possessions and information as much as possible. These agencies and advisors are not arresting the problem from happening in the first place. They advise the consumer on minimizing the possibility of having it happen. Once it happens, they offer suggestions and defensive actions to try to keep the problem from escalating beyond some form of control. Scaryyy!

The FBI, the Secret Service and Congress are overwhelmed with the prolific growth of identity theft and its related crimes. Compared to the out of control acceleration of identity theft, Congress and its agencies are moving at a snails pace in reducing the use of our social security number by both public and private businesses. The social security number is *THE* main target of every identity theft ring. More than eighty percent of social security number misuse reported to the social security administration's hotline was related to identity theft. The social security number is the major identifier of every

American in the United States. It's prolific use, increases your chances of having your number used for unlawful activity. Many state agencies would like you to believe that the American identifier is the driver license. Although a form of personal identification, your driver license number alone will not give an impostor the opportunity to attain every other bit of information about you. Try using your driver license number as your main identifier in college, or your doctor's office, or your insurance office, or with your banker or your investment broker, or your creditors or on your tax returns. Your social security number is required to receive service from almost any doctor or hospital throughout the country. If you inform them that you have no insurance coverage, the response is routinely, "Well, we still need your social security number." Your social security number is typically used as your employee identification number in every major corporation. It is the student's identification number in almost all state universities in the country. Thankfully, through much lobbying, some universities are changing this practice however; it is still big business with business. No one seems to be addressing the tremendous amount of service related businesses that now require this number before rendering the most basic of services. Service businesses ask for and expect to receive it on demand. If you want cable service, phone service and utility service be prepared to furnish your social security number before service is connected. It is difficult if not impossible to refuse many of them. Yes, you might find alternatives to cable but can you operate without telephone, water and electric power? Theoretically, your social security number should not be requested except by an employer, government agency, lender or credit bureau. Nevertheless, if you refuse to give these companies your number, they typically refuse you service. Therefore, what real *choice* do you have? Understandably, business is trying to protect themselves from consumers who do not pay for the services rendered them. With the correct social security number, the business can furnish both collection agencies and the credit bureaus with the bad debt information. Once demanded and received, both government and business put the burden on YOU, to try to protect the very information, (the social security number), that is required before service, employment or education is rendered. This is the very number that is desired by businesses and thieves alike. Once your number is out there, no one can promise protection. The government and business do not have to live with the repercussions of your information falling into the wrong hands. Only you do. Most recently, the wrong hands are those of identity theft rings or groups of thieves that do not find it as profitable to hit one person at a time. They like to "get inside" a company or persuade an employee already working for a company, to download the personal information of hundreds or thousands of employees or customers from databases and sell the blocks of personal information to crime rings for some big bucks. These quite organized, efficiently run, rapidly growing rings have the FBI and the Secret Service extremely concerned. Scary enough?

Chapter 8

The 3 C's:

- ## Creditor
- ## Collection Agency
- ## Credit Reporting Agency

Your education to become competent in your new job as Chief Executive Officer would not be complete without understanding a little more about the ways that credit grantors, collection agencies and credit bureaus or credit reporting agencies interact.

Credit Grantors: You are most likely well acquainted with credit grantors. Simply put, credit grantors or creditors are people or businesses to whom money is owed. Creditors typically use credit bureaus to establish the credit worthiness of prospective customers thus lowering their risk of extending credit to those consumers that have proven to be unreliable. Today, many creditors have internal collection agencies.

Collection Agencies: Collection agencies employ workers or "collectors" that contact debtors and attempt to collect money from them. If repeated attempts to collect fail, collectors may turn to the court system where they try to collect the debt through a judgment and may in fact, garnish wages. Most collection agencies pay their employees a salary and a commission based on the amount of money they collect. The more money the collector collects, the more money the collector earns. Therefore, the incentive to possibly hound and harass is typically, more money in their pocket. The Fair Debt

Collection Practices Act was adopted to try to stop abusive practices of collection agencies. Among other provisions, this law requires that a collection agency provide information to debtors and limits the ways in which a collector may try to collect a debt. Many states have additional laws that further restrict the activities of collection agencies. Chapter 14 gives you a brief overview of the provisions of this act therefore I won't go into it here however; I would like to clarify one area of this act that cause many of my clients confusion.

I will attempt to explain the confusion as best I can. Keep in mind that if you have specific problems with a collector, it can be advantageous for you to attain an attorney that specialized in the Fair Debt Collection Practices Act. The confusion most often raised by my clients lies in the thirty day dispute period. If a consumer notifies the collection agency in writing within 30 days of the collection agency contact that they dispute the debt and wish the collector to verify the debt, the debt collector must verify the disputed debt within the 30 day period. They must mail the verification to the consumer. The collector can be doing other things with the debtor's file during this dispute period. They do not need to stop their collection efforts within this 30 day dispute period, they just can't do anything to hamper *the debtor's right* to dispute the validity of the debt. Many of my clients believe this dispute period is a grace period and that the collector is prohibited from acting on the debt. It is important to understand that the 30 days is given to debtors as a dispute period and not as a grace period.

The business of collections has become so precise that the small generic mom and pop type of collection agency can utilize the collection service departments within some credit bureaus to help identify, locate and verify people they feel have outstanding debts. The credit bureaus can inform the collection agencies of the debtor's ability to pay. Some credit bureaus help a collection agency determine which debtor files to assign, which files they might consider selling or which files they might want to purchase. Some credit reporting agencies, (credit bureaus), even manage the mass mailing of collection letters for the collection companies.

Credit Reporting Agencies a/k/a Credit Bureaus: Many people got used to calling them credit bureaus but today they are most often referred to as credit reporting agencies. In writing, they are frequently referred to as CRA. The Federal Trade Commission oversees the activities of all credit reporting agencies. Credit reporting agencies gather pertinent information *about you* over your lifetime. The file of information they gather and maintain is called your "credit report". Some agencies and insiders refer to them as "consumer reports". I guess it sounds less menacing. It's the "kinder and gentler" name for *credit report*. Your credit report consists of things like your address, your employer and information about your bill paying behavior. Your file may also include any criminal activity such as if you've ever been arrested. It may indicate law suits. It also may indicate if you ever filed for bankruptcy, have judgments or tax liens. It does not include information such as your salary, insurance information or medical conditions. Each file is maintained *individually* therefore, you may be married and hold credit in both names but you each have individual files. *American* credit reporting agencies maintain credit files on United States consumers only.

The credit reporting agencies sell your information to businesses that want to know if you are a good *credit risk*. When you request credit, it is added to your credit report so that creditors can see your payment history and determine if you are a good credit risk. It is an accomplishment to maintain a good credit history over your lifetime.

When someone requests your credit file, an "inquiry" is added to your report. Not all inquiries appear on copies of your report furnished to various creditors however; your copies always include a list of current inquiries so that you know who has been viewing your report. Many inquiries are labeled with a description of why the report was viewed.

I am not going to get into credit ratings except to mention that the amount of "inquiries" you have from creditors are tied to your credit rating. Credit ratings estimate the amount of credit that can be extended with limited risk to individuals or businesses.

Therefore, if you are deemed "credit worthy" or a good credit risk, you most likely have an acceptable credit rating.

There are three national credit reporting agencies, Experian, Equifax and Trans Union. Each of the three national credit reporting agencies are independent of the other. There are hundreds of smaller credit reporting agencies. Many small credit reporting agencies are affiliated with the national credit reporting agencies. With the tremendous growth of identity theft, many companies are springing up offering to "monitor" your credit report and alert you to inquiries and activity. These companies are NOT credit reporting agencies. These companies typically describe themselves as information service companies. They can not alter your report in any way. They can only monitor activity on your behalf and with your express permission. (Why anyone would give even more people or companies access to their personal information is beyond me nevertheless, it is a matter of personal choice).

It would be naive to believe that the only services credit reporting agencies provide are credit reports. Each of the three national credit agencies collect and store information on over two million credit consumers and over 10 million businesses. Credit reporting agencies are in the information business and having all that information has given credit reporting agencies reason to be well diversified. They offer numerous services both to consumers and particularly to businesses. Credit reporting agencies often appeal to businesses by promoting the idea that to be successful in targeting the right consumer with the right offers, they must identify the consumers' preferences as to specific interests and lifestyles. My company recently received an unsolicited booklet advertising targeted sales leads from one of the three national credit reporting agencies. Within the booklet, the CRA advertises that their information on consumers can provide businesses better insight. They offer to help by providing information allowing businesses to target specific consumers, markets and resources. Many times their large databases can offer information and demographics necessary to assist certain businesses with specific decisions such as whether they should build in one particular area over another. Some offer businesses the opportunity to target customers that have a better ability to contribute to the businesses bottom line. The CRA encourages establishing relationships with particular customers and businesses that can increase their chances of profitability and lower their exposure to customers with unknown credit risks.

Chapter 9

Quiz to Determine Your Vulnerability

Take the following quiz to help determine what behaviors you may need to change to make yourself less vulnerable to having your personal information compromised. Don't forget that even if identity theft has already happened to you and you've successfully recovered, it can happen again. There are specific behaviors that we may do that increase our chances of being targeted. It is important to guard your personal information effectively. The following are simple yes or no questions. The score box appears at the end of the quiz.

1. Do you ever leave your purse or wallet in an unattended car?

2. Do you place outgoing mail and bills in your home mailbox?

3. Do you have check re-orders delivered to your home mailbox?

4. Do you receive unsolicited pre-approved credit card offers in the mail?

5. Do you throw out unsolicited pre-approved credit card offers before shredding them or tearing them into shreds?

6. Do you have too many different billing cycles-that would make it more difficult to detect if bills don't arrive for payment when they should?

7. Do you carry credit cards, insurance cards and information in your wallet that you'd be unable to list, should it be necessary?

8. Do you carry credit cards in your wallet you haven't used for months?

9. Do you still carry your social security card around with you?

10. Do you carry your checkbook in your wallet, purse, pants pocket or briefcase?

11. Do you have your complete name and address on your checks?

12. Does your employer use your social security number as your employee identification number?

13. Have you neglected to request your credit report within the last two years?

14. Do your name and address appear in the telephone book?

15. Do you write your account number on your check when paying your credit card bill?

16. Do you simply toss unshredded credit card, debit card and ATM receipts in the trash to dispose of them

17. Do your credit card companies fail to verify larger than usual purchases by calling you?

18. Do you purchase goods or services on-line?

19. Do you bank on-line?

20. Do you file your taxes on-line?

21. Do you toss empty prescription bottles away without removing the labels?

22. Do you give your credit card to restaurant workers that disappear from your view?

23. Do you make purchases without paying attention to the actual swiping of your credit card?

24. Does your bank or credit card company make changes to your account without requiring a personal identification number (PIN) or password? (Mother's maiden name does not count as a password).

25. Do you store personal information on a hard drive of a computer hooked up to the Internet?

26. Do you open e-mails from unknown sources?

27. Do you participate in telephone surveys when you don't know the caller?

28. Do you ever complete warranty information?

29. Do you enter contests requiring personal information?

30. Do you sign merchant guest books that ask for your name, address and phone number?

31. Do you give your social security number to service businesses that simply ask for it?

32. Do your name and personal information appear in college alumni books, newsletters, etc.?

33. Do you complete paper applications or forms - never inquiring what they do with your written information after it's input into their computer database?

34. Have you applied for a car or home loan or refinance lately?

35. Have you neglected to *Opt Out* with the three national credit reporting agencies, Experian, Equifax, and Trans Union to remove your name from marketing lists?

Scoring: Add the total number of yes answers you have.

6 or less: You should be commended. In today's society 6 or less affirmative answers are actually quite good. You are aware of the potential risk associated with making your personal information readily available and take preventative measures.

Between 7-12: You are walking the line. Although you are aware of the potential risk of having your personal information too available, you fail to take enough preventative measures to adequately protect yourself.

13 or more: You are not properly guarding the very information identity thieves seek. You must make conscious behavioral changes to help protect your sensitive personal information.

Chapter 10

Ways within Your Power
to Help Minimize Your Vulnerability

Now that you've taken the vulnerability quiz and consciously acknowledge some behaviors that you may do that increase your exposure, let's explore some more ways to minimize your vulnerability. I previously mentioned that you can try everything within your power to try to keep your personal information from getting into the public domain and the hands of unscrupulous people but that in today's society, keeping your personal information private is very difficult and at times impossible. That does not mean that you shouldn't try very hard to protect what IS within your power to try to protect.

Everyone who seriously wants to minimize their chances of having thieves easily target them should consider the advice and the following steps. No one gets up in the morning thinking that today is the day someone is going to target me for criminal activity but it does happen. Identity theft occurs everyday to thousands of unsuspecting people. If you take measures to avoid some of the behaviors associated with this type of theft, you can minimize your vulnerability. We know that thieves search garbage looking for personal information. We know that thieves steal mail from home mailboxes. We know that telemarketers call and request personal information. Moreover, we know that just because it happened to you once, does not mean it can't happen again. However, you CAN make it more difficult for thieves to target you easily.

1. Cancel all credit cards that you haven't used in 6 months. Open credit is a prime target for thieves. If you haven't used the card in six months, you probably

don't need the card and you certainly don't need the exposure.

2. Empty your wallet of *extra* credit cards. If you know you won't be using more than one or two credit cards, leave your other cards at home. Never carry your social security card with you. Most adults have their number memorized. Don't carry any identifiers you do not need. Don't carry your birth certificate, social security card or passport, unless absolutely necessary.

3. Make a list of all your credit card account numbers and bank account numbers (or photocopy front and back of cards) with customer service phone numbers and keep the list in a safe place. (Do not keep your list on the hard drive of your computer if you are connected to the Internet. Simply keep it on paper or a computer disk.)

4. I know this is inconvenient to do because carrying your credit cards in your wallet makes them easily accessible. Carry your credit cards in a separate compartment of your purse rather than your wallet. If thieves get your wallet, they don't necessarily "get your cards." For men, it's a little tougher. Remember the fewer cards, the better.

5. This is a behavior you need to retrain yourself to do. Keep your eyes on your credit card at all times. Don't give your credit card to a restaurant worker or anyone else that can disappear from view. Get up and follow your card. If you can't see your card, you don't know what's happening to it.

6. After paying bills, don't leave the envelopes containing your checks in your mailbox for your postal carrier to pick up. Bills should be mailed from the post office or

dropped in a traditional postal service mailbox. If you decide to ignore my advice and leave your bills in your home mailbox, NEVER raise the flag indicating there is mail awaiting pick -up. It raises the attention of more than your mail carrier.

7. When paying your credit card bills, it is never a good idea to write your credit card account number on your check. (Even when the merchant or creditor requests that you do so). It may be convenient for their accounting department but it is not in your best interest.

8. You can't just tear up a credit card to cancel it. You must call the issuing creditor and cancel the credit extended to you. Ask for a letter confirming the cancellation and request the creditor mail a closed account letter to the credit bureaus asking for your account to be labeled "closed by consumer."

9. Keep your credit card receipts in one place. Do not constantly misplace them. Although many states now have laws prohibiting your entire account number from appearing on a receipt and smart companies print only the last four digits of your credit card number on their receipt, many companies still print the full credit card number. Get used to looking at your receipts. Never throw out a receipt without tearing or shredding it.

10. If a person calls you at home or at work and you don't know the person, never give them your credit card number or any personal information. If they tell you they are one of your credit grantors, i.e. your Visa account company, think nothing of telling them you'll need to call them back at a time more convenient for you. Call the telephone number that you know is the true number and not the telephone number provided

by them and ask for that person. You can then decide what information you want to provide. Provide only information that you believe is absolutely necessary.

11. It is not a good idea to use the following as personal identification numbers (PIN): last four digits of your social security number, your birth date, your mother's maiden name or anything else that could be easily discovered by thieves.

12. Memorize all your passwords. Try not to use your mother's maiden name as a password. Even if they ask for it, tell them you need to use another word of authorization. Your mother's maiden name is easily accessible from public records.

13. If you've been a victim of identity theft and ordered new credit cards, never use the same passwords or personal identification numbers, (PIN).

14. Never give out your credit card number online unless you are purchasing an item from a well-known and secured site. Remember that there is no reason to give your credit card number for a free trial period of anything.

15. Always review your credit card invoices upon receipt reporting any unauthorized purchases or discrepancies to your credit card issuer immediately. Time is a critical factor in reporting unauthorized activity.

16. When paying a merchant by credit card, don't let them write your address, telephone number or driver's license number on the receipt. Your signed card should be sufficient and for additional identification

purposes *only*, they may ask to *"view"* your driver license.

17. Buy a document shedder and make it easily accessible. Use it to shred any document that has your personal information listed on it including unsolicited, pre-approved credit offers, receipts, or tax information. When a shredder is not available, get used to tearing all mail into pieces before tossing.

18. **SOCIAL SECURITY** numbers are the primary target of identity thieves. When you are asked to identify yourself at schools, employers, etc., ask to have an alternative to your social security number. Unfortunately, many institutions use your social security number, as your *identification number.* Many companies and schools have recognized the risk to their employees and students and are actively changing this practice or are printing only the last four digits of the number on all documentation.

19. Do not put your social security number on your checks or receipts. If a business requests your social security number ask them why. If you do not feel it is a legitimate reason consider telling them no. Ask to use an alternative number or be prepared to walk away. Your social security number should not be requested except by an employer, government agency, lender or credit bureau. If a government agency requests your social security number, there must be a privacy notice accompanying the request. Don't forget that if your social security number falls into the wrong hands, it can be used by someone to impersonate you in order to steal from your accounts or to steal from others in your name.

20. Learn to check your W-2 for extra earnings. It could indicate that someone else is employed under your social security number.

21. Don't give your checking account number to people you don't know. The numbers at the bottom of your checks and deposit slips called MICR numbers, identify both the routing number of your bank and also your account number.

22. Guard your checkbook. Reveal checking account information only to merchants and businesses you know are legitimate.

23. You must report lost or stolen checks immediately. Do not wait. Time is a critical factor in proving liability.

24. Properly store or shred canceled checks and old checks from checking accounts. You should always store current checks in a safe place.

25. Don't carry your checkbook with you if you only use your checks to write month end bills from home.

26. Don't leave large blank spaces in the number and amount lines on the checks you write.

27. If you do not have time to reconcile your checking account when your statement arrives, it is still important to *open and scan* your bank statements for any unusual activity as soon as your statement arrives. There is a time limit on your liability when alerting a bank to fraud.

28. You should only order checks that contain security features.

29. Do not have your check reorder delivered to your home mailbox. Always have them delivered to your bank's main location and personally pick them up. (It may be inconvenient but having someone steal 100 blank checks will be more of an inconvenience, believe me!)

30. Do not leave your ATM receipt at the ATM machine. Dispose of it by tearing or shredding.

31. Learn not to provide information that isn't required. For instance, most information requested on a warranty registration form isn't necessary for the warranty. If you decide to complete a warranty form, limit the information provided.

32. Never toss empty prescription bottles in the trash before removing the labels.

33. Watch out for fraud on the Internet. Scam artists work the Internet too. Just because it's advertised or posted on line doesn't mean it's legitimate. Be very cautious about giving out credit card numbers and other personal information. Even if you believe "many people are doing it." Many people are being ripped off and scammed too!

34. It is not a good practice to post genealogies on the Internet. Americans interest is growing in this area. The problem occurs when you reveal too much personal information. Most thieves seek sensitive personal information such as mother's maiden name, place of birth, birth date, etc.

35. Think twice before registering your personal information in order to VIEW a website. You should not be asked to do this simply to visit the site.

36. Every computer that connects to the Internet should have current virus detection software.

37. Contact your representatives and legislators when you feel strongly about additional protection needs and privacy rights. They represent you. It takes five minutes by e-mail.

38. Review your credit reports at least once a year to ensure that there have been no unauthorized accounts opened in your name or under your social security number.

39. You should "Opt-Out" to remove your name and information from the major commercial marketing databases by calling: 1-888-5-Opt-Out (1-888-567-8688) [Explanation of the term Opt-Out appears in chapter 3]

40. Make a habit of placing the following statement on the bottom of any letters, applications, and warranty cards,(if you feel you must complete warranty cards) and any other document containing sensitive personal information.

THIS DOCUMENT CONTAINS SENSITIVE PERSONAL
INFORMATION.
SHRED BEFORE DISPOSING

Changing behaviors or habits that you've had for years is not easy. However, it is important to realize that times have changed and you must change with them. It became apparent after September 11 that our entire country is at risk when identities are so easily falsified or stolen. We must do more than just alter our behavior in the hope of avoiding the criminal activity associated with identity theft. There are innovative technologies available that can make falsifying documents, credit cards and identities more difficult. As with all innovation, money is often needed for research, development, production and purchase. Consumers and businesses need to consider seriously the ramifications of not improving antiquated systems and products. Realizing that the innocence we once had is forever lost along with the notion that American soil and people are untouchable, should lead us to more realistic views of the changes that need to be made to re-enforce both our personal and national security and safeguard our way of life.

Chapter 11

Turning Procrastination into Perseverance: Creating Your System

Identity theft victims often experience overwhelming feelings. Feelings of anger, frustration, violation, helplessness and disappointment are just a few that I experienced and many of my clients complain of enduring. These feelings are normal. You have been the victim of a crime. To react unemotionally would be abnormal so it's important to acknowledge that your reactions are normal for the situation. Victims of violent crime often have physical signs that they have been attacked. You too, have been attacked. The signs of your victimization are just not as obvious. Unlike the violent crime victim dealing with the emotional, psychological and physical aspects of the violation, you will endure the emotional, psychological and *financial* aspects of your violation. (Many identity theft victims also experience a very physical reaction to the trauma as well).

It is important for you to acknowledge the feelings you are experiencing so that you can work through them. It is necessary to deal with the financial side of the crime immediately to help avoid serious damage to your financial standing and credit history. I can't stress this enough. Time is a critical factor in this crime. Time is important when notifying the creditors of your victimization. Time is critical when filing the police report. Time is significant when notifying financial institutions. Time is especially relevant to avoid having fraudulent activity or judgments appear on your credit reports. It is easy to become confused and overwhelmed with the amount of information and documentation you need to supply.

Creditors' calls and notices can engulf you. You must try to keep your head and emotions separate. Although *you know* you are a "victim," one of your biggest jobs is convincing the creditors, collection and credit reporting agencies that you are "a victim." You will be better able to resolve the problems you encounter if you follow a *system*atic approach that allows you to prioritize, stay organized and remain proactive.

Create your identity theft *File and Journal*

An organized system is the first step toward successfully proving your victim status to merchants, creditors, collection and credit reporting agencies. It is essential that you be organized and systematic when you begin accumulating data. Depending upon the severity of your identity theft, you will be making lots of copies! If you own or have easy access to a copy machine, lucky you. (If you use the copier at work, don't leave any personal documents behind). For those of you who own a personal fax machine that has the ability to copy, that will work too. However, if you do not own or have access to some form of copy machine, you might want to seriously consider purchasing a small new or used copier. Most of the copies you make will not come from your computer therefore a simple computer printer will not suffice.

We begin by creating THE FILE BOX. The file box holds EVERYTHING dealing with your incident of fraud. Keep EVERYTHING, everything, everything that has anything to do with your identity theft in one place for quick and easy access. All hard copies and original documents, correspondence, envelopes, notes, affidavits, police reports, notices, credit reports, etc., are to be located in the FILE BOX.

Include a notebook within your file that will be used as a journal to record and document all pertinent data such as company names, employee names, titles, departments, telephone numbers, extensions, dates, times, conversations, notes, etc. Do not write any information on individual slips of paper to be added to your journal at a later time. All information and notations are to be written and documented in your journal. It has been proven many times that he who has the best documentation is more likely to win this battle. Many people want to keep their journal entries on their computer. This sounds like a good idea and an easy way to document activity however, most of us won't go to the computer to enter a brief one-line notation. Before long, you're jotting notes of unexpected phone calls or brief conversations on slips of paper to be entered into the computer at a later time when access to the computer is easier. Soon your file box is full of little slips of paper that must be organized and entered into your "computer journal." That becomes a job in itself. Believe me...I do this for a living. Your system requires handwritten journal entries and notations. It's important *not* to make your journal complicated or too structured. Keep it user-friendly. When you need it, grab it and jot the information down. Don't worry about form. Just get all the information. If you do this, you should never have a problem finding the information you need, when you need it.

As you accumulate files within your file box, keep them organized in alphabetically order. Within your file box, begin accumulating information according to company name, i.e. Sonny's Pizza, Experian Information Solutions, Meteor Corporation, etc. Keep all notices received from Sonny's Pizza and all correspondence you mail Sonny's Pizza in one file folder labeled Sonny's Pizza for easy reference. (Correspondence you mail may <u>also</u> be saved in a file on a computer disk under say, "Identity Theft Correspondence." When you print your correspondence for the recipient, you will always print a hardcopy for your file box too. You will attach your hardcopy of the letter to any original correspondence and its postmarked envelope. Place all in the file box with the rest of the information and documentation for that particular company. In this example, your letter, etc. will be filed within the file folder clearly labeled Sonny's Pizza. At any time, you can easily locate ALL activity with any company to include the envelope with postmark indicating the date you received their correspondence, the correspondence, your letter of response, the listed documents you included with your response and any other pertinent information you received or sent. (It is important not to have half the Sonny's Pizza file on computer and half in the file folder. You can keep your computer-generated correspondence in a computer file but you MUST print your hardcopy for both the recipient and your file folder). When your correspondence is merely confirming the information discussed in a telephone conversation, place that correspondence in the file folder labeled with that company's name. All future activity with the company should be placed in that file as well. All additional correspondence and documentation such as the police report and all other law enforcement documentation, US Postal Service forms and correspondence, Social Security Administration forms, etc., will be placed in separate files within your file box under the appropriate headings.

Remember, the key to keeping a well-organized filing system is to have everything you need at your fingertips. It is too confusing and time consuming to have the creditor's correspondence to you in your file box and your correspondence to them in your computer. It would require your taking too many steps in order to locate needed information. When you save any computer-generated correspondence, do so on a disk or floppy and not your computer's hard drive. Some of your correspondence will include sensitive personal information that you don't want accessed by hackers and through viruses. (A key reason for keeping everything well organized and easily accessed is that you need to assume that you will have to re-mail a lot of previously mailed documentation and correspondence. This occurs for a variety of reasons. You do not want to reconstruct each letter or notification with appropriate documentation each and every time).

a) **Telephone calls**: Jot down the important information of each call in your journal. Find out to whom you are speaking. Ask for the company name. If you don't understand it, ask them to s-p-e-l-l it. Note the telephone number, the date, the time and the important details of the conversation. Follow every significant telephone call with written correspondence confirming the details of your conversation. If you include important copies of supporting documentation in your letter; make sure you mail it certified, return receipt requested. Staple your copy of the certified receipt to your copy of the letter and place it in your file box.

b) **Mail:** Open all mail right away and staple the correspondence to its envelope and place on top of your file box. You do not have to *read* the letter upon opening it. You don't have to get into the details of every notice or letter upon its arrival. However, definitely open and remove the letter from its envelope. You will easily notice when the letters are piling up and you are "procrastinating." It also keeps you from dreading a pile of unopened envelopes that you know carry nothing but bad news.

Creditor and Collection Letters: Answer creditor and collection letters within 2 to 3 days of their arrival. Don't let the creditors' letters pile up. The growing mound of letters will quickly become intimidating. Remember, time is a critical factor. This is not the time to procrastinate. Additionally, creditors typically give you ten to fifteen days to return completed forgery affidavits. Like it or not, you should allocate a *minimum* of one hour a night to your identity theft problem. Depending upon the severity of your identity theft, you may prefer spending a few hours over each weekend devoted to your identity theft. Allocate your time effectively. The important point is that you take care of answering all correspondence in a timely manner. Remember, we are turning *procrastination* into *perseverance and persistence.*

Sample letters are available in chapter 16. After answering each notice or letter mailed to you, clip or staple together your certified receipt, your reply letter, the creditor's correspondence and their envelope with postmark and file in your file box. When saving the hard copy of the correspondence you wrote, don't *continuously* copy the supporting documentation you include with each letter. It's unnecessary paper documentation. You will know what items you included with each letter by looking at the enclosures you listed after your signature. *This will be made clearer in item # 7.

d) Credit Reports: You will receive copies of your credit reports from each of the three national credit reporting agencies when you place fraud alerts on your files. Keep the credit reporting agency information, (information from Experian, Equifax and Trans Union or their affiliates) in separate files labeled with the names of the credit reporting agency.
**You will handle credit reports, correspondence, and supporting documentation with the credit reporting agencies as a separate process using the information you have gathered in the files above.

e) Forgery Affidavits: Keep copies of forgery affidavits within the file folder of the company that had you complete it. Even if you are using a standard forgery affidavit, keep a copy of the affidavit you sent within the file. If you don't copy the affidavit that you mailed, you will be left to assume that you must have included the standard forgery affidavit because the company's specific form is not present. Don't assume anything, make a copy.

A Detailed & Organized PLAN

Let's review why we need a plan. Under the present system, countless identity theft victims must continually prove their innocence regarding fraudulent claims, acts and activity performed in their name. Victims must often defend themselves to the very creditors that extended the fraudulent credit. The plan to try to prove that you are innocent of incurring the debts and opening the accounts is a two-part process. In part one, you must determine what fraudulent activity has taken place, notify all the entities involved that you were a victim of financial fraud, try to stop further fraudulent activity, cancel all fraudulent accounts and collect the documentation or proof, supporting your victimization. (For informational purposes, I have assumed that nothing has been done and we will start the process from the moment you realized you are a victim of identity theft or fraud).

In part two, using the supporting documentation you have accumulated, you must try to have the unauthorized and inaccurate information that may appear on your credit files with the credit reporting agencies *removed* or *corrected*. Ideally, each creditor to whom you prove the account fraudulent, should send the credit reporting agencies notice to correct or remove the inaccurate information from your credit file. Unfortunately, this does not always happen. On occasion when the creditor does notify the CRA, the CRA just...doesn't remove it. (Why? I'm clueless). On other occasions, the CRA does remove the fraudulent accounts but some of these accounts mysteriously reappear three months later! On yet other occasions, some credit reporting agencies remove the inaccurate information and others do not. Soooooo, we will always ask the creditor for a copy of what we ask them to send the credit reporting agencies so that when things go wrong, you can DO IT YOURSELF. Let's begin with the first of the two part process. As you read each process, remember that I am providing a "guide" and you must individualize the suggestions according to your particular fraudulent circumstances.

Process One:

1. File A Police Report and Obtain A Case Number
Except for Internet fraud, most instances of identity theft should be reported to the police department where you believe

the theft occurred. If you are not sure, report the theft to your *local* law enforcement. Get the case number assigned to your report.

It's important to get the name of the officer who will handle your case, their card, their department and a phone number and extension where they can be reached. (The case number is often conveniently written on the back of the officer's card).

> The police report and case number are crucial pieces of your supporting documentation. Ask for the case number right away. A copy of the report may take a few days and is not imperative. The *police case number* is evidence indicating that you have filed a report and are truly the victim of a crime. It is generally required by merchants, creditors and collection agencies when proving your victim status. Without the police report having been filed, you could be labeled as just another scammer trying to get away with not paying your bills. Unfortunately, many people, for one reason or another, choose not to pay their credit card bills. Therefore, you must be able to prove that you are not one of these people but truly a crime victim.

2. Notify all Credit Card Companies ASAP

Immediately telephone your credit card companies and cancel accounts that have been compromised. If you become aware of *new* credit accounts fraudulently opened in your name, telephone those credit grantors. Creditor notifications must be made immediately to stop your liability and so the creditor grantors can limit their exposure and stop issuing credit under the accounts. It is essential to record the date you notify each creditor as well as the name of the representative to whom you speak. (Remember that the person who has the most verifiable documentation has the best chance of preventing further complication and of correcting inaccurate information that may later appear on credit reports). Most customer service representatives will only give you their first name. That is fine. Record the following information:

- credit card company name
- representative's name and department (example: fraud department, customer service department)
- the phone number and extension number
- the date
- any confirmation number they give you
- brief summary of conversation
- follow-up your verbal notification to the credit grantor (credit card company) in writing
- request a letter from the credit grantor confirming the closing of the fraudulent accounts.
- ask the creditor to send a notice to the credit bureaus notifying them the accounts were closed due to fraud. You should request the creditor's confirmation letter and notification to the credit bureaus when you contact them by phone and again when you follow-up in writing. Their sending the fraudulent account information to the credit bureaus is instrumental in having the account's erroneous information deleted from your credit report.

The credit grantors will ask you questions regarding your knowledge of the fraudulent accounts. Tell them everything you know about the fraudulent account. They will most likely request you complete an Affidavit of Forgery. They will mail their specific form to you for completion. They will ask you to mail all information and documentation you have verifying and supporting your claim of fraudulent account activity along with the notarized forgery affidavit.

a) **If you don't know your credit card numbers:** Go through your checkbook registry to figure out which companies' cards you have and go through old bills to find the telephone and account numbers.

b) **Replacement credit cards:** Do not have the credit grantors mail replacement credit cards to your home address if thieves obtained that information too. Many identity thieves steal mail right from your home mailbox. If they suspect you are receiving new cards, they can easily steal those too. Credit card companies love to issue your replacement cards immediately. It is all right to wait a day or so to order the replacement cards. In the mean time open a post office box and have replacement items delivered there. Many times thieves are privy to many personal details of your life including exactly where you live. If you have your mail delivered to your home, they could very well steal future mail. Don't have new credit cards and checks delivered to your home mailbox. Consider having replacement credit cards delivered to your new post office box. Have new checks delivered to the branch of your bank. They routinely accept responsible for your checks until they are in your hands. Do not place outgoing mail in your unattended home mailbox.

Establish a security feature with your replacement credit card accounts. Ensure that any changes to your account or requests for new cards are authorized by you in writing or by phone using an established password. (Don't use a former password).

c) **Account status**: After you cancel the compromised cards or after notifying them of fraudulent accounts opened in your name, ask about any recent requests for additional cards, address changes or any other changes to your account or under your social security number. Inform them immediately of all activity you did not authorize. Always, follow up your notification of unauthorized changes (such as address change) or activity in writing. If you have informed them in a timely manner, Federal law dictates your *maximum* liability to the credit card companies is $50 per card on unauthorized charges.

3. **Notify ALL three national credit reporting agencies immediately.**

Call the fraud division of the three credit reporting agencies and notify them you have been a victim of identity fraud. If you have recently lost your personal identification and do not yet know if anyone is committing fraud in your name, it is best to notify the three national credit reporting agencies and place a fraud/security alert on your file.

Experian	**Equifax**	**Trans Union**
PO Box 596	**P.O. Box 105069**	**P.O. Box 6790**
Pittsburg, PA	**Atlanta, GA 30368**	**Fullerton, CA 92634**
(800)-311-4769	**(800) 525-6285**	(800) 680-7289
www.experian.com	www.equifax.com	www.tuc.com

a) **Ask that a <u>Fraud Security Alert</u> & a <u>Victims Statement</u> be added to your credit file**.

All three national credit reporting agencies have automated fraud lines to call. Each agency has their own system for handling such calls. An automated voice will inform you that a fraud security alert will be added to your credit file if you have been a victim of fraud or suspect that you are a victim of fraud once you furnish them with the required information. They will ask for your social security number, street address, year of birth, telephone number, etc. The personal information is required to add a fraud alert to your file. This alert **REQUESTS** credit grantors (companies looking at your report to determine your credit worthiness, example: credit card companies), to verify your identification prior to extending credit. A fraud or security alert typically stays on your file for a mere 90 days.

Remember that one of your *goals* is to make it uncomfortable for your impostor (s) to continue impersonating you. You are trying to create roadblocks so that they discontinue using *your* personal information. One of the most important actions you can take to try to impede or stop further fraudulent activity is to add a **Fraud Victim Statement** to your credit file. The victim's statement stays on your file for 7 years and ideally, you are **asking credit grantors to contact you at the phone number you supply before extending ANY credit in your name and under your social security number**. This security measure is much, much better than the 90 day security/fraud alert. The phone number you give can be home or business. This statement will also prevent YOU from obtaining instant credit because you must be at the phone number you provide the credit reporting agency to verify that the credit extension is authorized. Having said that, I cannot imagine ANYONE that has experienced true identity theft, wanting *instant credit* available to them.

The obvious downside to the **fraud/security alert** is that it only stays on your file for 90 days and does not protect you as much as the fraud victim statement. A downside to the **fraud victim statement** is that it is not immediate and you must mail or fax the credit bureau a *paper document* containing more sensitive personal information. The information requested includes your complete name, previous addresses, social security number, date of birth and your spouses name and social security number, along with a copy of a document such as a phone bill or utility bill verifying your name and address. What happens to this paper document after the credit reporting agency enters the information into their database is anyone's guess. However, you don't have a choice. It is vital to add the 7 year fraud victim statement to all credit files of identity theft victims. Neither the fraud/security alert nor the fraud victim statement will stop credit grantors from hounding you with unsolicited offers of credit. And none of this matters when companies extend instant credit with no credit verification. Cellular phone services are notorious for doing this! Internet providers frequently extend credit without credit verification. With the explosion of this crime and its potentially devastating repercussions, I think it would be a great idea to consider ways of prohibiting *instant credit with no credit verification. (*I don't know why it's not an immediate red flag to creditors when consumers are afraid of having their credit verified). I can tell you hundreds of stories about unverified credit histories that have led to crimes perpetrated against the innocent

Experian boasts having the best consumer fraud assistance and I believe that to be true. Their fully automated system is quick, easy to understand and follow with little if any, problem encountered. They offer the added benefit of removing your name from marketing lists for solicitation purposes during the same phone call. As an added security measure, to date they appear to be the only agency that DELETES your social security number from the mailed copy of your report. Both Equifax and Trans Union mail copies of reports with the social security number clearly visible for anyone to see including anyone that fraudulently requested the report, received the report in error or were faxed the report. Experian's report is easy to read and understand, has good instructions to follow should you find inaccurate information and includes a user friendly form with each report to notify them of inaccuracies. Additionally, once my clients have notified the three credit reporting agencies of the fraud perpetrated against them and anxiously await the three credit reports to determine what fraudulent activity has transpired, Experian's credit report is almost always the first report my clients receive.

Although we live in a technological society, there may be times when the automated systems of the credit reporting agencies go down. After asking you to enter all the required personal information through your phone line, you may receive a message informing you that the automated system is not presently available! When this has happened, the Equifax automated system actually requested my clients **FAX** their personal and sensitive information. FAX! I never recommend faxing sensitive and personal information. Again, this may be convenient for business but is it safe for you? Both Trans Union and Equifax have actually asked victims to fax a copy of their social security card and driver license, their full and complete name, current and former addresses, date of birth and a copy of an official document also containing their social security number! ***Can you possibly imagine anyone who has or is experiencing thieves fraudulently using this very information, faxing it for anyone to receive or better yet, mistakenly receive?*** I have often received faxed documents intended for other destinations. And even if all your personal information makes it to the desired destination, where does it all end up? There could be pieces of you floating all over the credit bureau. It may be convenient for the credit reporting agency but it is not in your best interest. I suggest you never *fax* anything containing personal and sensitive information.

b) A copy of your report will be mailed to you free of charge.

By federal law and upon request, you are entitled to one free copy of your credit report every 12 months when you report that your file may be inaccurate due to fraud.

Once received, you will notice that your report consists of activity that hopefully, has been generated by you as well as names of various companies that have inquired about your credit worthiness and /or your credit rating. Carefully review any activity that is unfamiliar to you. Examples: loans you did not request, unfamiliar addresses, unknown names or aliases, accounts you did not open and any unusual inquiries made to your account. Remember it is important to periodically request copies of your report from each of the credit reporting agencies so that you stay alert to any additional fraudulent activity. I usually suggest requesting your reports at least every six months after you've been victimized. Disputing unauthorized information that you find in your credit reports is explained in Process Two in the next chapter.

If you find fraudulent credit activity on your credit report that you were unaware of, call the creditor that extended the credit immediately. Notify them about the fraudulent account.

4. Call Your Bank And Report The Incident.

Cancel all ATM, bankcards and debit cards that are missing, being used fraudulently or you believe may be compromised. Do not have your new replacement cards mailed to your home mailbox. Either have your bank hold them for your personal pick up or wait until you have arranged for a post office box and have them delivered to that address. See CHECKS below, if your checkbook was also stolen. Record the date, the bank representative's name, their title, their department, their phone number, any confirmation number they give you. If you meet in person, make sure to get their business card. If you are a victim of someone using your social security number fraudulently but your bank cards are not missing or stolen and have not been compromised, you should still notify your bank that you are a victim of financial fraud and request that your account be PASSWORD protected and ask about additional security features they can attach to your accounts. Always confirm your notifications in writing.

5. Cancel all compromised phone cards, gasoline cards, merchant cards, library card, pharmacy cards, video store cards, AAA card, membership cards, check cashing cards, employee id cards and any other card you believe may be compromised.

Depending upon your incident of fraud, if you believe any of the above cards have been or might be compromised, cancel them immediately. Many companies have toll-free numbers and 24-hour service to deal with emergencies. Once you report the loss or theft in a timely manner, you have no further responsibility for unauthorized charges. Be sure to document the day, time and to whom you spoke. Confirm your notifications in writing.

Remember, under federal law, your *maximum* liability to the credit card companies notified of unauthorized activity in a timely manner is $50 per card.

6. Federal Trade Commission website

Visit the Federal Trade Commission website. It is easily accessed and is an excellent source for referrals, resources and suggestions, for hotline and other phone numbers, addresses of agencies, information on state identity theft laws and links to other useful sites. Additionally, the FTC has created a standard Forgery Affidavit available for downloading that covers new accounts opened in victims' names that a number of creditors accept. www.consumer.gov/idtheft.org

7. Complete Affidavits of Forgery:

There are situations in which your bank, the credit reporting agencies and various credit card companies need to verify that *you* are not responsible for incurring the outstanding debts and that you are truly a victim of identity fraud. You might be asked to provide proof that you did not create the debt by signing statements under oath that you did not make or authorize the fraudulent activity. This document of proof is known as a forgery affidavit. Each company may want you to complete and have notarized its *own specific* affidavit. (Many will take a copy of a standard affidavit. It just depends on the company's policy). After completing each affidavit, it is important to make a copy for your file. Should creditors write you a second or third time, copy them with the previously sent affidavit. Always mention the date you mailed them the original information.

As I mentioned earlier, the Federal Trade Commission is diligently working on uniform methods of notifying businesses and organizations of identity theft activities. One of the methods is providing proof of your victimization through a *standard* forgery affidavit that they call the *ID Theft Affidavit* available for downloading through their website. You can copy this standard identity theft affidavit and send it to many different companies. The ID Theft Affidavit asks you to furnish a lot of information. Determine what information the creditor needs. If you decide not to complete certain areas of the affidavit and intentionally leave any area blank, be sure to write NOT APPLICABLE in the space so the company knows you did not mistakenly skip the question. Presently only certain companies with *new accounts* opened in your name accept this affidavit.

8. In the case of Check Fraud:

If you know or suspect that you may be a victim of check fraud, you still need to obtain a police report and case number. Notify your banking institution immediately. In all probability, you will be asked to call a 1-800 number and report the incident to a customer service center representative that might be located in a *central customer service center* half way across the country. Explain in as much detail, everything that is pertinent to them assisting you.

➢ They need all pertinent information to file the appropriate documentation with their insurance and investigators (and to relieve you of suspicion).
➢ You will be asked to complete one or more affidavits of forgery.

Every banking institution will suggest ways of preceding that are specific to their financial institution and fraud policies and your particular incident of fraud however, the basic scenario should follow general guidelines similar to the following:

a) Stop any overdraft protection you may have in place. Once thieves deplete what was originally in your checking account, overdraft protection can continue to fund your checking with your savings or money market balances.

b) Inform your bank of all outstanding checks that have not cleared. Your financial institution might work with you on allowing only those checks to clear and no others. They may advise you to leave enough money in the account to cover the outstanding checks. Once the checks clear, the account will be closed. (Again, there are a number of alternate ways to fund your outstanding checks and close the account. Check with your specific financial institution).

c) Open a new checking account. Some people choose to open their new account in a different bank. (I chose to do this to better distinguish between the fraudulent checks and my new account. All new checks ordered on your new account should include security code features). Make sure your account is password protected. Ask your bank to label your old account specifically as *Closed Due To Fraud*. This immediately places all creditors and merchants on notice when the fraudulent checks are returned to them stamped *Account Closed Due To Fraud*.

d) Should you choose to close the original account right away and all your legitimate checks, (checks **you** have written), have not cleared, you might consider calling the entities that have your legitimate checks and explain that your account has been closed due to fraud and you will issue them a replacement check from your new account.

*You may incur banking fees if your legitimate checks are presented and returned to the creditors as insufficient funds or account closed due to fraud. Your financial institution or creditors may work with you on this. If they do not, pay any fees and keep an accurate accounting of your out-of-pocket fees in your identity theft file.
** Your accountant may be able to assist you with the unreimbursed financial losses incurred as a direct result of your identity theft.

e) When ordering your new checks, alter the appearance of your checks to distinguish them further from your closed account. Limit the amount of personal information printed on the check front. Don't print your entire legal name. Women should reconsider printing both their maiden *and* married names, i.e. Mary Smith-Brown. Some people decide to use only initials such as M.S. Brown. You might consider printing your post office box on the check front instead of your home address. One advantage to doing this is that should your checks ever be stolen, creditors, merchants and thieves will not obtain your home address from the checks themselves. Do not have your home phone number *printed* directly on the checks. When asked by a merchant to supply this I, either tell them that I do not give out that information or I supply them with my office phone number. **NEVER** print your social security number on your checks. Many people in the military do this. This is really looking for trouble and is no longer a viable action.

**Even though a post office box appears on the front of your checks, your actual account and all related information can still be under your home address. Your monthly statements can still be mailed to your home address or personally picked up at the bank. (Again, consider having statements and cancelled checks delivered to your post office box that remains locked until *you* open it.

f) Once all required financial documents and forgery affidavits are completed and you have filed a police report and received the case number, the bank will be able to summit your file to their insurance investigators. After a proper investigation and according to your specific incident of fraud, the financial institution should reimburse any money fraudulently taken from your account to you in a timely manner. Some financial institutions will give you provisional money or conditional money so that you can still pay your bills, etc. during the time it takes them to conduct a thorough investigation.

9. Checks that continue to be forged

After having completed all the steps I've mentioned, you may still experience checks that continue to be forged in your name. If you are a victim of check duplication, check kiting, check alteration, or other banking or check schemes, it may be awhile before merchants or banks stop accepting the fraudulent checks. It may be awhile longer before merchants and creditors stop looking to you for payment. If *your* name, address and telephone number were given along with the fraudulent checks, you may receive harassing phone calls and messages from creditors, merchants and collection agencies. As the fraudulent checks continue to be returned "account closed", the creditor's computers might automatically generate collection letters. After non-payment for a specific period of time, your account could be sent to a debt collector or collection agency. It is extremely important that you answer each and every merchant, creditor, and collection agency that write you seeking payment. If you do not advise them of your situation, they will assume you are responsible for having incurred the debt. Along with following the suggestions in item number 10 below, it is important you mail each creditor and collection agency specific details of the incident as it relates to them. Include the information contained in your *standard incident reply letter* along with supporting documentation that is pertinent to them. (The next chapter explains the *standard incident reply letter*). Keep in mind that time is a critical element in notifying the creditors and in keeping the situation from escalating beyond your control.

10. Notify the check verification companies.

Contact the companies that merchants and financial institutions use to verify check information as well as collect on returned checks. Below are phone numbers of some of the larger check verification companies. Call them and report your checks stolen or forged. Explain your circumstances. <u>Don't forget to follow up in writing.</u> Include your stolen or fraudulent checking account and routing number. In your letter, include pertinent information such as the police case number, forgery affidavit and bank representative name and phone number. After your initial call, the companies will put your fraudulent or stolen check information in their databases in an effort to stop future checks from being accepted. This is an excellent proactive step to take. Should the verification companies contact you in reference to future bad checks, explain that you have already notified them of the fraudulent checks and that the documentation should already be on file with their company. You can tell them that you will gladly resend the information if you can mail it to a *specific person's attention*.

- ❖ National Check Fraud Service: 1-800-571-2143
- ❖ SCAN: 1-800-262-7771
- ❖ TeleCheck 1-800-366-2425 or 1-800-710-9898
- ❖ Check Rite: 1-800-766-2748
- ❖ Equifax Check Systems:1-800-437-5120

11. Incident Information& Reply Letter
Because so many companies will require the same information regarding the fraudulent activity, it is time effective and efficient to copy your basic incident details and information supporting your victimization from letter to letter. Take your time when deciding on the information to include. Be sure to list the important and RELEVANT details. Once you are satisfied that the information provided is sufficient for creditors and others to investigate the account (s) as fraudulent, use your list of basic information in future correspondence and notices. Depending upon who you are contacting, the information you include will vary. Offered are some suggestions of what information to include.

Basic Incident Information
Include in all Reply & Notification Letters

- Your complete legal name

- The fraudulent account and the name appearing on the fraudulent account

- Your Social Security Number

- Refer to the police case number, the name of the detective responsible for your case, their address and/or telephone number.

- If your financial institution is involved, include the institution's name, the name of the person responsible for handling your account or investigation along with their phone number.

- If you are confirming contact to a creditor, include the account number, the name of the person you spoke with by telephone –(just include the first name if that is all they gave you), their department (customer service, fraud department, etc.).

- Refer to the enclosed forgery affidavit covering the fact that you have been a victim of fraud. (If this is a second or third letter to the same company, in the individual letter to the company, refer to previously sent letters and forgery affidavits).

- Refer to any additional *pertinent* supporting documentation you have included such as documentation from the postal service, DMV, banking documents, creditor letters, etc.

Example:
Identity Fraud Victim: John Q Public
Social Security Number   123-45-6789

Account in the name of: John Public
Fraudulent Account Number: # XXXXX XX XXXX
Financial Institution: Money Bank
Bank Representative: Mary Smith, Customer
                               Service Manager
                               (555) 555-5555 Ext. 123
Police Case number: # 4567
Detective & phone number: Det. Joe Jones, Any town Police
                               Department
                               (555) 555-1234 Ext. 45
Forgery Affidavit: Enclosed

Reply & Notification Letter

Incorporate your basic incident information in future correspondence to the different businesses and companies you must contact. In all reply letters, type the current date, the specific address of the company to whom you are writing, reference specific account numbers, previous correspondence, previous telephone contact, etc. In the body of your letter, use the relevant information from your list of basic incident details. ALWAYS include your original signature on every reply letter. Remember you are writing a *new* letter to each recipient and *incorporating* the basic information of the incident. You are eliminating the time consuming and repetitive act of typing the same incident information repeatedly to each entity that contacts you. The key to the success of your incident reply letter is to make it concise, no more than one page. It must only contain *pertinent and relevant information* related to your incident of fraud. You don't want to ramble on so that the recipient never finishes your letter. You do not want to write so much that they misinterpret or misunderstand the very purpose of your letter. There is a delicate balance of supplying enough information without getting into unnecessary details. It is important that you take a professional and serious position in each letter.

Always check spelling and grammar usage. It is a good idea to ask a friend or family member to read over your first few letters, making sure that your letters give the information needed and are easily understood. (You know all about your incident and the circumstances surrounding it but have you properly conveyed your information to someone reading it for the first time?)

Make a hardcopy of each reply letter you mail for your file box. For your reference, I have included a suggested outline of a typical reply letter. Each of your letters will be different depending upon the information supplied and the type of business you are notifying.

REPLY LETTER FORMAT:

- The current date and the specific address of the company you are writing. If you are writing to a specific person, include their name above the address.

- Double space down from the address and include as a subject, Re: Account # 123456 or whatever is pertinent in helping the recipient identify your account or the subject matter of your letter.

- In the heading of your letter and to the right of the address, clearly type the word CERTIFIED or REGISTERED. (If you have the certified slip already, include its number after the word certified.) If this is letter number two or more to the same company, document the other certified letter numbers as well.

- After your greeting, refer to the telephone conversation you had or to their letter that you are in receipt of dated such and such.

- In the body of your letter, include your <u>basic incident information</u>. (This is the information you include in each notification letter). *See <u>Basic Incident Information</u>* on preceding page).

- Be sure to sign each letter personally. Include the number of enclosures. It should be a minimum of one, your forgery affidavit, possibly more if you enclose copies of previous correspondence sent them and any other pertinent documentation.

- Mail all of letters certified, return receipt requested. Mailing it certified gives you additional proof that you sent them notice in a timely manner, gives you proof that they received it along with the name of the person that actually signed for your letter.

- Staple the following to <u>your copy</u> of all standard reply letters: the creditor's letter, the envelope it came in with the dated postmark and your half of the certified receipt. Place in your file box. Remember there is no need to copy your enclosures.

Many companies will mail you more than <u>one</u> standard form letter demanding payment. If the letters are from a collection agency, always try to respond to the creditor for whom the collection agency works as well as the collection agency. In any additional letters you mail to creditors and collection agencies, always refer to previously sent certified mail. Consider stating that you have furnished them with the necessary information and documentation on (state the dates) enabling them to investigate your incident of fraud. You may indicate that after having sent the necessary documentation, you do not expect to be further harassed by receiving additional letters demanding payment. Include copies of your previously sent notifications. You may choose to refer to the Federal Fair

Debt Collection Practices Act within your subsequent letters. Sometimes when you state that you are aware of the specific laws pertaining to your rights as they relate to the situation, your letter stands out and you are taken more seriously. Other times, it back fires and they just get irritated. You never really know the perfect strategy to take. If you feel that they are continuing to violate your rights, you may want to consider contacting an attorney and actually filing legal action.

This is a judgment call based on the facts of your situation however, should you find yourself having to write a third or fourth letter, you must determine if it is time to seek someone higher within the company to receive your information. If you do decided to do this, research the company and mail your correspondence to a specific person. This can be a powerful tool, do not over use it but do use it to your best and ethical advantage. Logically determine who might be the best person to help resolve your situation and mail them your information.

***Remember to always address each letter to the *specific* company you are writing. NO REPLY LETTER SHOULD BE COPIED AND MAILED OUT IN BULK FORM. The only information that is copied from letter to letter is the basic incident information.

11. Contact the Department of Motor Vehicles
If your driver license was stolen or you believe someone may be using your driver license number, contact your local DMV and report that you are a victim of identity theft and you believe someone may be fraudulently using your name and/or driver license number. Each state handles things differently. It is good to be on record that someone, somewhere may be using your name or driver license number with *their* photo as proof of identification.

12. Contact your Post Office
Contact your post office to report any incident of mail tampering, mail theft, mail fraud, etc. You can obtain additional

information by going to the United States Post Office Official website at: www.usps.gov. If you do not know how to contact your specific Postal Service, contact the United States Post Office at 1-800-275-8777.

13. Contact the Social Security Administration

Contact the Social Security Administration if you suspect that your social security number has been compromised or used illegally. Your social security number is the main target of identity thieves but it also holds the key to your history with many companies and government entities. Once you know your card or number has been taken or used, continually check items like your W-2 for extra earnings. Extra earnings could indicate that someone is employed and working under your social security number. Because your social security number holds so much historical information about you, the government is extremely reluctant to issue a new number. On very rare occasions and under extreme circumstances, the social security administration may decide to issue a new number however, if a new number were issued, the ONLY legal way to receive a new social security number is for **YOU** to talk to the Social Security Administration, personally. Anyone who promises they can obtain a new number for you is deceiving you. You may contact the Social Security Administration's fraud hotline at: 1-800-269-0271 or www.ssa.gov

14. Notify your State Attorney General's Office

This is optional. According to the degree of your victimization, it might be a good idea to write your State Attorney General's office and inform them about your identity theft. Your letter will be on record should any company also report you to their office. If you *do* notify your State Attorney General's office, you can include that fact in your letters to creditor grantors. You may want to mention that your incident of fraud is on record with your State Attorney General's office.

This is an easy piece of additional documentation supporting your victimization.

15. Consider changing your phone number
    If you are experiencing an undue amount of phone harassment, if your phone number appeared on the <u>front </u>of the stolen checks or if your phone number is published in the phone book, you may consider changing your existing phone number. Should you find yourself unjustly harassed by debt collectors, understanding the consumer protection outlined in the Federal Fair Debt Collection Practices Act might help you. *See Chapter 13 On Bills & Laws*

16. Consider other options
    Remember that each incident of identity theft is different. Depending upon the specific circumstances and severity of your situation, you may need to consider contacting other agencies and companies including your phone and utility companies, the passport office, and an attorney.

Chapter 12

Disputing Unauthorized Information Appearing on Your Credit Reports

This is the second part of the two-part process to try to prove your innocence and victim status in hopes of reclaiming your identity. Your credit report might indicate additional fraudulent activity that you had no idea occurred. We are going to use your report as a map or indicator to determine what other fraudulent activity has taken place that must be stopped. Then the report's misinformation will have to be corrected.

As I mentioned in chapter 8, your credit report contains information about you such as your name, address, social security number, your credit history, your credit rating, if you've ever filed for bankruptcy, been arrested, have judgments, tax liens or lawsuits along with any criminal convictions. Credit reporting agencies compile all this information and sell your report to businesses. Nationally, there are three credit reporting agencies, Experian, Equifax and Trans Union. As the population grows, these credit reporting agencies rely on smaller, affiliated and local credit reporting services. For example, in Central Florida, Experian uses a company called Credit Data Services, Inc. and Trans Union uses Merchants Association Credit Bureau, Inc. Many local companies are divisions or subcontractors of the national company. Businesses need, want and use the information contained in your credit report to evaluate your credit worthiness. Your file follows you recording the activities affecting your credit and credit worthiness over your lifetime! Due to this, it can be devastating when someone fraudulently uses your name, social security number, credit sources and credit history to open new lines of credit. Therefore, it is extremely important to notify the credit reporting agencies as soon as you learn you have been a victim of fraud. *Once information of any kind goes on your credit report, it is difficult to change.* Acting quickly and diligently, notifying creditors and following up on your notifications can help avoid fraudulent activity from appearing on your report and save you from an extremely time consuming and tedious pursuit.

a) Unauthorized Activity Found On Your Credit Report

Following step number 3 of The Plan, you notified all three national credit reporting agencies of your incident of fraud. Under federal law, you will automatically receive copies of your credit reports to review for inaccurate information and fraudulent activity. Immediately call the business or creditor noted on your credit report if you find NEW and open accounts on your credit report that you did not authorize or open. Notify the creditor that you are a victim of identity fraud and that the account was established fraudulently. Tell them you want the account closed right away and that you <u>need a letter from them confirming the account's closure</u>. Ask that they notify the three national credit reporting agencies of the fraudulent account activity and ask them to have the CRA remove all of the account information from your credit file. Don't forget to follow-up all creditor notifications and requests in writing. Most creditors will close the account immediately but might request you complete their forgery affidavit that includes a request for the police case number. If you have a completed and certified copy of the Federal Trade Commission's standard forgery affidavit, ask the specific company about sending that instead of completing yet another individual forgery affidavit. If the representative you're talking with doesn't know if that is acceptable, it is up to you to decide whether to mail it or wait for their affidavit to complete. As mentioned earlier, the FTC website has a standard ID Theft Affidavit that you can download and use to report information to companies that have established NEW ACCOUNTS in your name.

It is important that you document the name of the creditor, the name of the representative to whom you reported the fraudulent activity, the date you notified them, their department and the specific account information you supplied as fraudulently generated. Include this information in your Reply Letter and mail it along with your forgery affidavit and any other information you have that supports your victimization. It is crucial you obtain confirmation letters from the creditors confirming the closing of the fraudulent accounts and that the closings or cancellations were due to fraud. Creditors report activity to the credit bureaus. The credit bureaus will only correct the inaccurate information if they receive notice from the creditor. If the creditor does not follow-up for you and report the fraudulent account to the credit reporting agencies, you can be proactive and notify the credit reporting agencies yourself because you have a copy of the letter from the creditor confirming the account as fraudulent. Send the credit reporting agency a copy of the creditor letter along with the fraud affidavit. The CRA will typically use your furnished creditor letter to contact the creditor and the creditor will investigate your claim of inaccuracy due to fraud.

If you feel you supplied the creditor with the required amount of documentation to understand and investigate your claim of inaccurate or erroneous information but your claim is still denied, don't think it is you. This is not atypical and is a complaint voiced by many victims. Often after providing the creditor with all the required supporting documentation, the creditor may refuse to notify the credit reporting agency of the inaccuracy. At this point, continued correspondence to the same department is a waste of your time and effort. Faced with this problem in the past, I have mailed the well documented erroneous information to a higher authority within the same organization. You can also file a complaint with the FTC by contacting their Consumer Response Center. Although the FTC cannot resolve individual problems, they can act against a creditor or merchant if enough people report similar problems or a pattern of law violations is established.

Once you notify the CRA of inaccurate information appearing on your credit report along with supplying them with required supporting documentation to contact the creditor, you must be diligent in following up on the corrections and the removal of the fraudulent accounts from your credit reports. Upon receiving your information, the credit reporting agencies are supposed to investigate and remove unauthorized activity however, ninety percent of the assistance Identity Theft Management gives victims is in this specific area. It can be a tedious and time consuming process.

If the fraudulent accounts appearing on your credit report are already CLOSED due to say, delinquency or for any other reason, you must still notify the individual credit reporting agencies that those accounts were fraudulent. Those accounts are inaccurately appearing on your report and need to be deleted. Each credit report includes a form to report any inaccuracies. Be sure to attach your supporting documentation. The CRA will investigate the inaccuracies based on the information you provide. Supply enough detail and supporting documentation so that a thorough investigation can be done. Take your time and do a professional job. The easier you make the investigation for the credit reporting agencies, the more likely its removal or correction. All proven inaccurate information should be corrected or deleted from your reports. Ensure the CRA received your request to investigate by following up within ten days or send your information by certified mail. (After supplying the credit bureaus with such important and time-consuming documentation, Identity Theft Management always suggests its clients send the information to the credit bureaus by certified mail, return receipt requested). Be sure to request the action you want taken in both your cover letter and on the credit reporting agency's form. Additionally, request a copy of their investigative findings or a corrected credit report. To illustrate your cooperative efforts further, provide a daytime phone number where you can be reached to answer any additional questions they may have. See *Sample Letter To Credit Reporting Agency Disputing Credit Report In Chapter 16.*

b) The Frustration of Working with the Credit reporting agencies

Under the present system, identity theft victims typically find themselves having to prove their innocence regarding fraudulent activity performed in their name however, consumers and victims of identity theft have specific rights under the Fair Credit Reporting Act. Under this Act, the Credit reporting agencies and the organization that provided the information to the CRA, (perhaps a bank, credit card company or merchant), have a responsible to investigate and correct any <u>inaccuracies</u> or <u>wrong information</u> contained in your report. Upon supplying credit reporting agency with appropriate supporting documentation, they are supposed to investigate the items in question, usually within 30 days unless they consider the dispute to be frivolous. *After* investigating your claims, the credit reporting agencies have <u>no </u>specific period of time in which they must *correct* the inaccuracies so don't be surprised if it takes awhile. (Some agencies are better than others). Identity Theft Management comes to the aid of many identity theft victims after they supply the credit bureau with the lengthy, time consuming and tedious documentation disputing incorrect information on their credit reports, only to be left wondering if the CRA actually investigated any of the items in dispute! Frequently, all of the incorrect information continues to appear on their credit reports or in some cases, the inaccurate information is actually corrected only to reappear six months later! Again, this is not atypical. The FTC is aware that some credit reporting agencies occasionally refuse to cooperate with the victim trying to correct their credit report.

What makes the notifications to the credit reporting agencies even more time consuming and tedious is the fact that each of the three national credit reporting agencies are independent of the other and although federal law requires that they communicate corrections to one another, often times one credit reporting agency's credit report will have information not contained on another's. Plan to report the inaccuracies along with all your supporting documentation three separate times.

Be sure to include all relevant information enabling each CRA to conduct a thorough investigation otherwise, your request will be deemed frivolous. The credit reporting agency must give you a written report of their investigation. They will also furnish you with another copy of your credit report if the investigation resulted in changes having been made to your credit file. If their findings do not resolve the disputed item (s), you may request to add a *brief* explanation of the disputed item to your file.

If you truly believe your credit report contains discrepancies reported by a creditor or merchant, but the creditor or merchant denies your dispute, examine your supporting documentation. Did you include enough evidence so that the creditor's consideration was based on accurate information? If you did not provide concrete evidence to substantiate your claim of fraudulent activity, get more documentation and mail it again.

If you have truly provided all the documentation required establishing the fraudulent and unauthorized activities and the items are still not corrected or removed from your credit report, you may want to contact an attorney that specializes in the Fair Credit Reporting Act.

In addition, if you have been wrongfully accused of a crime or have civil judgments entered in your name due to fraudulent activity, it is time to seek legal counsel and legal advice.

Although an agency such as the Federal Trade Commission may investigate and stop suspected misconduct, the FTC will not be able to get you damages for the misconduct. You may want to consider speaking with an attorney about your rights under the Fair Debt Collection Practices Act and applicable state laws.

In your cover letter to the credit reporting agency, include:

1. Your complete name, address and daytime phone number.
2. A copy of your report with each disputed item clearly highlighted
3. A brief explanation along with facts as to why the information is inaccurate
4. *Copies* of all documents that support your claims or discrepancies
5. Your requested action
6. Mail the package certified, return receipt requested

See Sample CRA Dispute Letter In Chapter 16

Please know that only time can remove **accurate negative information in your report.

❖ Accurate negative information can stay on your report for 7 years.
❖ Bankruptcy information can be reported for up to 10 years.
❖ Criminal convictions have NO time limit.

See Sample Letter: *If an Item on Your Credit, Report Is Correct, But You Would Like a Statement Added for Future Creditors* in Chapter 16

Now you might better understand why it is so important to request your credit report periodically. If no adverse activity is taking place and you are simply verifying your status quo, there will be a nominal fee per request. It is well worth the money.

Chapter 13

What You Need to Know about Some of Today's Frauds and Scams

Scams and various deceptions to impersonate people and cheat them out of their money have been around for years. Today, there are more ways and means of stealing people's personal information and committing fraudulent acts then ever before. Credit card fraud, credit repair fraud, check fraud, banking and various financial Institution fraud, computer fraud, on-line banking and Internet fraud, and telemarketing fraud are seeing new and innovative schemes. The present technical revolution has created an alarming increase in the incidence of different types of financial fraud. As previously mentioned, the low cost and availability of high tech equipment make it available to all but a few. The very affordable high-resolution copies and scanners make the counterfeiters tools readily available. Before ready accessibility to this type of equipment, counterfeiting and check fraud was typically committed against big business. Today, it's committed against everyone. I've included information about just a few of these activities that might impact your daily life.

Credit Card Fraud:

I mentioned in an earlier chapter the latest and very prevalent credit card fraud known as "skimming." This is where dishonest restaurant workers, waiters and waitresses or merchants and store clerks can swipe your credit card twice without your knowing. Your credit card is swiped once to pay your legitimate purchase and then swiped a second time into a small portable credit card magnetic reader sometimes referred to as a "skimmer." After voluntarily turning over your card for payment, your card's magnetic strip with your account information is read and stored on this small reader and re-encoded onto any other card with a magnetic strip making that counterfeit card identical to yours.

Skimming is fast and easy. The crime has accelerated rapidly in the United States however, it is not limited to the U.S. Skimming has a foot hold in every major city around the world. The simple magnetic strip was never designed to guard against crimes using sophisticated technology. The simple magnetic strip can be copied to perfection. There is even a battery-operated hand held skimmer that has been developed that is small enough to fit in a pocket. It had a microchip able to store the data of at least 20 cards, which can be downloaded onto a laptop computer. With one swipe by a dishonest person, the details of the magnetic strip are stored on the skimming device. The electronic codes can be sent via modem anywhere in the world and then imprinted on other cards. It has become so prevalent that it is unusual not to read or see this type of criminal activity reported on the evening news. Many of the counterfeit cards are literally made thousands of miles away from your real card. International crime rings are said to even e-mail the codes. It is reported that organized crime rings here in the United States as well as crime rings in the United Kingdom, Australia, Italy, Hungary, Canada, Nigeria, the Czech Republic, Japan, and others are heavily involved in this type of crime. A scary fact is that the crime has escalated beyond the skimming device. Skimming bugs can actually be implanted in the *LEGITIMATE* terminals of your favorite merchants, department stores and restaurants! The crime has become much more sophisticated than the systems required to detect and defend against it. The sophisticated tools to combat this type of criminal activity have been slow in development as well as shunned by a society that places strong limits on acceptable forms of privacy protection. There is no denying however, that the magnetic strip on the back of credit cards has become antiquated and leaves us all vulnerable.

Reported over the business newswire was a story about a travel agent that was prosecuted for having used her customer's credit cards to try to rejuvenate her failing business. She was sentenced to 16 months to four years in prison and was ordered to pay almost $500,000 in restitution to more than 300 clients.

Credit Counseling Services & Credit Repair:

You can usually tell the difference between legitimate credit counseling services and others by the fees and promises they make. Legitimate credit counseling services usually charge nominal fees and work with a client to develop a plan to help them "re-establish" their credit. Bad credit counseling services and credit clinics on the other hand, often charge much higher fees. They may make promises they can't fulfill such as removing bankruptcies and liens from credit reports. As I have mentioned in an early chapter, only *time* can remove *accurate* information from a credit report. *Inaccurate* information, such as unauthorized fraudulent activity, can be investigated and corrected. Federal law mandates the amount of time negative but accurate information must remain on your credit report. **No one** can remove bad credit from a credit report simply because you pay them. Anyone who thinks they can pay someone to obtain a new credit report or new credit identity is being scammed and is actually involved in a popular credit-repair scheme. One scheme has you replace your social security number with a new "employer identification number" and a new bank account thereby, allowing you to believe you have a "new credit identity." People who follow this advice are actually violating federal law by using false identity on credit applications. This is as bad as using someone else's social security number on an application. It is against the law.

My company, Identity Theft Management spends a tremendous amount of time helping identity theft victims understand the major differences between idle credit repair promises and what rights your government has given you concerning inaccurate information appearing on your credit reports due to fraud. Everyday we receive numerous calls from identity fraud victims asking about credit repair services and their ability to help repair credit. Identity theft victims that have <u>inaccurate</u> or <u>incorrect</u> information appearing on credit reports due to fraud, don't need the promise of a *new* credit report. You need to CORRECT your credit report and have the inaccurate information investigated and removed. You can do this yourself by following the instructions that came with your credit report, by following the advice appearing in this book or by asking for guidance from legitimate agencies and companies like Identity Theft Management. As previously mentioned the credit reporting agency, Experian includes an easy form to follow right in with your credit report. Consider using their form as a guide when notifying the additional credit bureaus. The most difficult and time-consuming part of completing the report is supplying the information that supports your victimization and then ensuring that the incorrect information is corrected. If you have followed the advice and the credit reporting agency continues to report the inaccurate or fraudulent accounts, make sure that you supplied the necessary documentation to adequately support your claims. They will not just make changes to your report simply because you ask. They will not make corrections to your report based on flimsy excuses, long involved stories or poor documentation. If you feel that you have supplied adequate documentation to support the information as inaccurate or erroneous and they still deny your requests, it may be time to seek outside assistance or a legal professional.

Don't ever be tempted to pay a debt that you did not incur simply to get the debt paid off and closed on your credit report. If the debt was truly incurred through fraudulent means, you have a right to have it deleted from your report. I had a client who did this. He went to a bad credit counseling service and they suggested it would be easier for him to "pay-off" the small account opened by his identity thief than to try to prove to the creditor and then the credit reporting agencies that he did not open the account or incur the debt! It might have been less time consuming yet, it took its toll in other ways. Not only did he have the expense of the debt and the expense of the credit counseling service and its bad advice but the credit counseling service now appears on his credit report. Many people don't realize that often times when a debt is paid-off *through* a credit counseling service, the fact that the debt was paid through the credit counseling service may be noted on the credit report. This information could stay on your credit report for up to 7 years. (Also very few credit counseling services tell you that they can sometimes receive as much as 75% of their funding from creditors. So, who has their loyalty the client or the creditor?)

If any victim receives notice of legal action based on debts incurred through the fraudulent use of the victim's personal information, it is time to obtain legal assistance. Don't ignore legal notices!

Check Fraud:

Check fraud schemes take many forms. Your checks can be altered, counterfeited, forged, and drawn on accounts you've closed. Check fraud costs financial institutions millions of dollars if not detected early. In addition to direct financial losses there are many substantial hidden costs associated with this crime, including investigations, audits, legal fees, insurance, employee time and employee training costs that are eventually passed on to the YOU.

You, as well as your financial institution, need to be educated and aware of some of the most common of check fraud schemes. It is essential that tellers and other financial institution personnel be able to recognize common characteristics of check fraud. Financial institutions must realize that their personnel are often the first line of defense.

The financial community should ensure that all its employees are educated on various check schemes and in-place internal policies to help curb the devastation this type of fraud inflicts on both their institution and their customers. There are wide varieties of check fraud. The following are just a few schemes:

> Altered Checks: A criminal uses chemicals or some other means to erase or alter the information written on a legitimate check. They can enter their own name as payee or change the dollar amount. An Internet protection company recently illustrated a simple example in their newsletter. They mentioned how important it is to complete as much of the payable section of your check as possible. They used the example of people that find they owe the IRS money and must write them a check. The Internet protection company suggested writing out the entire name of the *Internal Revenue Service* rather than simply writing the acronym *IRS*. Simply writing initials leaves room for scam artist trickery. Scam artists can alter the "I" in IRS with a few simple strokes, thereby changing the "I" to an "M". The check that was payable to the "IRS" is now payable to "MRS."…whom ever they want!

> Closed Account Fraud: Closed account fraud occurs when checks are written against closed accounts. This type of fraud typically occurs when criminal's count on the float time between two different banks. It's important that you destroy checks of closed accounts. Let's say your checks are stolen so you notify your bank and they close the account but the criminals deposit some of your stolen, closed account checks (checks representing "0" funds) into a new account at a different bank through the bank's ATM. The float time between the ATM deposit and the checks drawn on the closed account reaching the issuing bank for payment can allow the criminals

time to withdraw money (that does not exist) from the new account. This is known as check kiting.

➤ Counterfeit Checks: The quality of today's generation of computers, printers, scanners and desktop publishing software has made document fraud attractive to a wide variety of criminals. Crimes like check-counterfeiting offer the criminal a low cost, low risk of apprehension and high economic gain potential. This crime has accounted for billions of dollars in losses to consumers and businesses. Many times the same desktop software publishing programs legally used to create your own checks are used illegally to counterfeit various financial instruments. Criminals obtain a genuine check and scan the check into the computer. The criminals can change the date, the payee, the dollar value of the check, corporate logos, any number of other features. They print the check on check paper obtained from any office supply store. The result is a high quality counterfeit check that is virtually indistinguishable from your real check. These same methods are used to print counterfeit birth certificates, social security cards and more. One way to help deter criminals from using computers and accessories in this way is for financial institutions and various businesses to utilize higher security measures. You may be familiar with one security measure that many merchants employ. Do you remember seeing SCAN written on the side of the register the last time you went shopping? Have you wondered what that means? SCAN is an acronym for shared check authorization network. It is used by participating banks and merchants to check for any previously bad account activity. It works by having participating financial institutions report all checking accounts that are closed for cause to a central database. The company operating the central database then transmits the closed account information to the shared check authorization network database. This is one reason why I suggested victims of check fraud proactively notify the check verification companies. *See Chapter 12.*

Alone, the following signs may mean nothing out of the usual yet, often times when combined, these signs can indicate that a check *might* be counterfeit:

> The check numbers are low
> Four smooth edges (Most checks will have at least one perforated side)
> Visibly different print fonts used on the face of the check
> Staining or discolorations on the face of the check possible indicating alterations
> MICR numbers at the bottom of the check don't match information on the rest of the check. This is quite common
> Information printed in unusual areas
> Limited information is provided such as printed address but no phone number, name but no address, no bank name

Counterfeit Driver licenses and fake ID's:

Phony driver licenses of the highest quality are readily available and out there. Aside from daily news of DMV thefts of licensing equipment, advanced technology also contributes substantially to the proliferation of this crime. The high quality computers and their document scanners and copiers make this crime easy and common. Phony driver licenses are often undetectable by the best law enforcement officers. Fraudulent checks and credit cards are then supported by fraudulent identification...fake driver licenses.

Banks & Financial Institutions:

The majority of financial institutions are better prepared to handle fraud within and against their institution, than they are fraud against their customers or account holders. The financial sector's defense against many types of fraud lies with developing and using cutting-edge technology notably in the field of biometrics. By combining proper identification through authentic documentation and the matching of fingerprints, face geometry, eyes, etc., we can greatly lower opportunities for fraud. We must consider and adopt new and innovative answers to the criminal's activities.

My clients continually complain about the way their financial institution treated them when they reported fraudulent activity regarding their accounts. Some were told that the bank or credit union they had been going to for years couldn't help them and they'd have to go home and call an 800 number! These frightened and confused crime victims were told to basically fend for themselves. They got little if any, information or guidance on how to proceed other than the 800 telephone number. I believe most of this is due to not having an "in-place" system to handle financial customers in these situations. With the tremendous amount of identity theft victims reporting their theft to financial institutions, it is a sad commentary that most of their personnel still do not know the basic assistance and information to offer identity theft victims. Instead of acting unattached and not a part of their account holder's problem, they must become part of their customer's *solution.*

Financial institutions also need to ensure that changes to customer's accounts are legitimate. They should always require customers use passwords or PIN's that guarantee the identity of their customer when requests to change account information is made. In addition, it's a good idea to have financial institutions limit the size of cash transactions at branch offices and require customers (or possibly their impostors), to complete large transactions at the customer's main banking location. Although sometimes inconvenient, there is a better chance that there are more personnel at the financial institution's main location trained in recognizing fraudulent activity than in the smaller staffed branch offices.

Computer Fraud:

As previously discussed, there are thousands of ways today's criminals use the computer and the Internet to perpetrate fraud against the average, unsuspecting consumer. Computer experts say many people are enticed into opening e-mails sent them that contain computer viruses that can give the hacker access to your entire computer system. In addition, hackers often *trick* Internet surfers into visiting interesting and enticing websites that contains viruses and worms, thus gaining access to their computer system. If you bank online, have your resume online, shop online, file taxes online, the hacker and anyone they sell your personal information to can impersonate you. If they obtain your password or PIN, they could break into your bank account!   Never send any sensitive personal information by e-mail.   The average person's e-mail is not encrypted and can be seen by many. Many businesses use technology like Secure Socket Layering (SSL) to encrypt today's Internet transactions making the website a little more secure. This technology encrypts the information you send and usually the information you may receive back. Coupled with firewall protection, sites with SSL advertise secure websites. Every hacker will tell you that nothing is guaranteed safe but SSL is the latest in today's encryption technology for electronic transactions. You typically know that the web page you're visiting is encrypted if you see a small lock icon at the bottom of the page. If you see nothing or an open lock, assume the information is probably not secure. I visited the website of a well known women's business association and some of the web pages that asked for personal information were secure however, other's were not. I think that most people assume that all the site's pages must be secure if some are secure. That is not the case. If you do not see the locked icon at the bottom of the page, do not forward your personal information.

In addition to the security features, you may want to determine if the website saves your credit card information after you purchase the product. If you can enter your credit card information, switch to another page and retrieve your information upon returning to the original page, it's cached within their system. It is usually *not* cached, (not stored) if it is gone after you enter your information and before saving, switch to another page.

On-line Banking:

People who find it convenient to bank on-line need to realize that the Internet is a public medium and the prospect of unauthorized access to personal information by the criminal element is very, very real.

Individuals with access to Internet codes can perpetrate a multitude of on-line fraud using the identities of other people. A recent investigation into an account takeover scheme resulted in the arrest of a bank employee who retrieved bank customer accounts, changed the customer's mailing addresses and sent newly issued credit cards with the customer's true identities to himself.

Internet Fraud:

When criminals use the Internet to commit their crimes they have access to a huge population as well as virtual anonymity.

Sensitive personal information about Internet subscribers and shoppers are often innocently stored in unsecured databases, which can be accessed through poorly protected websites. When customers access goods and services through the Internet they are exchanging the goods for payment by way of electronic transfer of credit card information as well as some personal information. Through badly designed and unprotected databases, hackers can get into websites and downloaded credit card information from people who have made purchases. The innocent subscriber or shopper rarely knows that they have had their credit card or bank account compromised until they receive their statement weeks later. By then, their credit history can be destroyed. In other cases, hackers have been known to gain access to customer accounts by using passwords known by employees of the merchant or website.

Knowing the amount of credit card and personal information that has been intercepted and "hijacked" when sent over the Internet unencrypted has given rise to the idea of purchasers swiping their card at home. This would be one way of combating this type of Internet fraud. Purchasers would swipe their credit card at home, the same way a merchant does in the store. The equipment plugs into your keyboard and encrypts your card's information before entering the computer system. The goal is to keep your credit card information and personal information off your hard drive. (A variation of this idea is already in-place in some restaurants. The diner swipes their own credit card at the table instead of giving the credit card to a server who disappears).

You've probably seen the words *Privacy Policy* on hundreds of Internet sites you visit. Do you really understand why it can be important to know the site's privacy policy? Many, many sites collect and use information about you just by your visiting that site. It's a good idea to become familiar with the types of information websites collect and what these websites do with the collected information. (You can stop wondering why you receive so much "e-junk mail" or "spam")

Telemarketing Fraud:

Telemarketers may call you, ask for, and receive your personal information. The need to use both caution and skepticism cannot be stressed enough. You can no longer afford the luxury of giving people you don't know your personal information. Today it is very important to exercise caution and skepticism when dealing with people that are unknown to you. Dishonest telemarketers are out there. Some may call you. We read and hear stories of unscrupulous telemarketers stealing money through the unauthorized use of credit cards but they can also gain access to your money through unauthorized withdrawals from your checking accounts. The scenario goes something like this: A telemarketer calls and explains that you have won a free prize. If you respond to the offer, they usually ask if you have a checking account. If you answer positively, the telemarketer explains the offer. The offer is usually too good to be true but in fact, they called you and aren't you the lucky one. Toward the end of their amazing one time only offer, the telemarketer asks you to read the numbers from the bottom of your check. They make up various reasons why they need this information. A fabricated reason could simply be that they are making the offer through a banking association and they must make sure that you hold a legitimate checking account with a major financial institution. Once the telemarketer has your checking account information, they can write up a *demand draft* and send it to your bank for payment. The demand draft contains your name, your account number, and any dollar amount they decide on. This type of draft typically does not require your signature. When your bank receives the draft, the amount is withdrawn for the dollar amount specified on the draft and paid to the telemarketers' bank. Again, you won't know this happened until you receive your next bank statement. Had you simply said goodbye and promptly hung up or told them that you do not give out any personal information over the phone, you would have received the best prize of all...you would have kept all your money and your personal information!

The National Fraud Information Center is a nationwide hotline to obtain information on telephone solicitation and possible telemarketing fraud. You may report telemarketing fraud to them as well. They can be reached at 1-800-876-7060 or www.fraud.org

REMINDERS

❖ Do not give any personal information to a website that asks you to "pre-register" before allowing access to their information. They often ask for your email address, phone number and/ or address. Many times the information YOU supplied is gathered and sold on mailing lists.

❖ Do not <u>volunteer</u> any personal information to unknown persons. If you are contacted by phone or e-mail and asked to update your credit card information for reputable companies such as AOL, AT&T, and Discover, don't assume it's really a representative from those companies. YOU call THEM back at a number you obtain from your bill and inquire as to what they need updated on your account and why. YOU make the phone call to a phone number YOU obtain. Many scammers have sophisticated ways to appear as if they represent large companies with whom you may be doing business. They often ask and receive your personal information. I suggest everyone attending my identity theft presentations and seminars alter their behavior to help minimize their chances of having their personal information compromised. They complain that *not* supplying personal information is difficult in our society. I always tell them and I will tell you to *treat your personal information as if it were money because it means money to your identity thief and it might take a lot of your money…to try and get back!*

Chapter 14

Some Pertinent Laws
that
Might Help You

It is important be aware of the various laws that govern you and the laws that pertain to your rights relating to personal information and identity theft. The laws are changing daily. Since September 11, our legislators realize that there are too few laws governing the misuse of our personal information. I have provided a very brief overview of some pertinent *federal* laws that are currently in place. You can obtain the complete law as written from a variety of sites on the Internet including the Federal Trade Commission's website. In addition, each state is busy creating and passing bills governing their residents. It is important to know the various *bills* that are up for approval in both your state's legislature as well as our federal legislature. You can make your voice heard by calling or writing your representatives and letting them know your feelings pertaining to specific bills. Most states realize the impact the crime of identity fraud is taking on their residents. The Governor of Florida organized a special task force to address privacy and technology issues. Based on recommendations by this task force, the Florida legislature is considering a number of bills, two of which would increase penalties for criminals convicted of serial (repeated) fraud schemes. According to Bill SB540, *if* convicted these criminals *could* face up to 30 years in prison, a $500,000 fine and ordered to pay restitution. Another bill dealing with the misuse of our personal information is SB1040; it would prohibit merchants in the state of Florida from printing more than the last five digits of a credit card number or from printing the expiration date of a credit card on an electronically generated receipt given to the cardholder. Many other states already have this law. You should become aware of what laws relating to public information and privacy govern your particular state. The bills are a start however, we must then have the system in place to actually arrest the offenders, prosecute them and order jail time!

In too many states catching and prosecuting identity thieves is a low priority for police who very often have a single detective assigned to economic or financial crimes. The Secret Service and the FBI investigate identity theft and fraud however, they concentrate on big money cases and fraud rings, not individual fraud losses. As most identity victims know, it is not atypical for career identity thieves who actually are caught and convicted to spend very little time in jail. This remains a crime where the potential payoff is usually worth the risk. The only people that can help change this pattern of injustice are the very people it is happening to, you! There are enough of us to demand that the punishment fit the crime. There are an estimated 800,000 of us annually! Enduring years of ruined credit, stolen identities, time consuming phone calls, letters and reports, tolerating constant identity confusion and unwarranted encounters with law enforcement agencies, possible misrepresentation of social security earnings and no sense of financial or psychological security should be a crime with very specific and commensurate consequences. Be aware of the bills before your state and federal legislatures and when you hear of one you agree with, e-mail, fax, write or call them and let them know you are behind them! It takes five minutes.

The Freedom of Information Act (Very brief overview)

The Freedom of Information Act (FOIA) was passed by Congress in 1966. The FOIA specifies that the public owns the information and data that is in trust with the government on both the state and federal levels and that information is available to the people accept where restricted by law.

Agencies of the United States government are required to disclose records upon receiving a request for them, except for those records that are protected from disclosure. This right of access is enforceable in court. The federal FOIA does not provide access to records held by state or local government agencies or by private businesses or individuals. All states have their own statutes governing public access to state and local records. Congress amended the FOIA statute in 1974 and most recently, the **Electronic Freedom of Information Act Amendment of 1996 (EFOIA)** expanded the scope of the FOIA to include electronic records and to require the government's creation of "electronic reading rooms" to make records more easily and widely available to the public.

The Identity Theft and Assumption Deterrence Act of 1998 (The Identity Theft Act) (Brief Overview)

The identity Theft Act addresses identity theft in two ways. First, the Act strengthens the criminal laws governing identity theft by making it a <u>federal crime</u> to knowingly transfer or use another person's identification without lawful authority and with the intent to commit or to aid, any unlawful activity in violation of Federal law or under related State or local laws.

Second, the law focuses on consumers as victims. Prior to the law only financial institutions and creditors were considered victims because they were the ones that sustained monetary losses. Under the Identity Theft Act, consumers are considered victims as well due to the harm to their credit and credit history. Among other things, the Act directs the Federal Trade Commission to log the receipt of complaints by victims of identity theft against credit reporting agencies and credit grantors, to provide identity theft victims with informational materials and resources, and to refer complaints to various entities, including the three national consumer reporting agencies and law enforcement agencies. For a full description of this act and its provisions visit the FTC website.

The Fair Credit Reporting Act (FCRA) (Brief Overview)

The Fair Credit Reporting Act, was established to help protect consumers by allowing them to seek remedies against inaccurate or incomplete credit reporting. It establishes measures for correcting errors and inaccuracies on your credit report. It also requires that copies of your report are made available for *legitimate* business purposes only.

The Act protects information collected by consumer reporting agencies such as credit bureaus, medical information companies and tenant screening services.

Companies that provide information to consumer reporting agencies also have specific legal obligations, including the duty to investigate disputed information. Entities that use the information for credit, insurance, or employment purposes must notify the consumer when an unfavorable action is taken due to the report. Companies that provide information must be identified within the report, so that the accuracy and completeness of the report may be verified or contested by the consumer. Information in a credit report is not supposed to be provided to anyone who does not have a specific and *legitimate* business purpose. The Federal Trade Commission is responsible for enforcing this act. For a full description of this act and its provisions visit their website.

The Fair Credit Billing Act (Brief Overview)

The Fair Credit Billing Act establishes procedures for resolving billing errors on your credit card accounts. This is also the Act that limits a consumer's liability for fraudulent credit card charges to $50 per card. This Act amends the Truth in Lending Act. The Fair Credit Billing Act requires prompt **written acknowledgment** of consumer billing complaints and investigation of billing errors by creditors. You must write the creditor about billing errors within 60 days of having received your statement indicating the error. It prohibits creditors from taking actions that adversely affect the consumer's credit standing until an investigation is completed, and affords other protection during disputes. The creditor must acknowledge your dispute within 30 days of receiving it and must resolve the dispute, one way or another, within 90 days. The Act also requires that creditors promptly post payments to the consumer's account and either refund overpayments or credit them to the consumer's account. For a full description of this act and its provisions visit the FTC website.

Consumer Protection Act (Brief Overview)

Congress passed the Consumer Protection Act in part to regulate the consumer credit industry. It requires creditors to disclose credit terms to consumers. The Consumer Protection Act also protects consumers from loan sharks, restricts the garnishing of wages. It established the National Commission on Consumer Finance to investigate the consumer finance industry. Credit card companies and credit reporting agencies are also regulated by the Act. The Act also prohibits discrimination based on sex or marital status in the extending of credit. The Act also regulates certain debt collectors.

The Fair Debt Collection Practices Act (Brief Overview)

The Fair Debt Collection Practices Act prohibits debt collectors from using unfair or deceptive practices to collect past due bills and debts. Many states have additional laws that further restrict the activities of debt collectors.

Under this Act (Title VIII of the Consumer Credit Protection Act), third-party debt collectors, (when a creditor hires another party or entity to collect debts on its behalf), are prohibited from employing deceptive or abusive conduct in the collection of consumer debts incurred for personal, family or household purposes. Today, many merchants and creditors use debt collectors to collect on their behalf because the merchant or creditors' expertise lies not in debt collection, but in selling goods or services or extending credit or loans, etc. They typically try to stay with what they do best and hire others to do what they are not in business to do. This Act requires collectors to provide certain information to debtors and limits the tactics that a debt collector may use. Some collectors have gone to unethical and unlawful lengths to intimidate and harass debtors. For example, collectors may not contact debtors at odd hours, telephone them excessively or reveal to others the existence of your debts. Our government realized that the consumer must be protected from these over zealous collectors who are often paid a percentage of the amount of money collected. The Act forbids a debt collector from calling you without identifying themselves or making false statements when trying to collect a debt or threatening legal action that is not really intended. This would include implying that you have committed a crime or that you are going to go to jail unless you pay them; Implying that they are attorneys or government representatives, if they are not; Representing themselves as employees of a credit reporting agency or threatening to file a report with a credit reporting agency. (Only the owner of the debt can file against consumers, not people working for the owners of the debt). They also cannot use profane language or threaten violence. They cannot threaten to garnish, attach your wages or sell your property unless the agency or creditor, (the actual owner of the debt), intends to do so and has taken legal action to do so. Sometimes informing them that you know your rights under the law, is enough to have them deal with you legitimately. The Federal Trade Commission is responsible for enforcing this act. For a full description of this act and its provisions visit their website.

**If you are experiencing this type of harassment, you can contact the Federal Trade Commission. They can be contacted at (202) 326-3222, www.ftc.gov or you can write them at Correspondence Branch, Federal Trade Commission, Washington, D.C., 20580.

The Electronic Fund Transfer Act (Brief Overview)
The Electronic Fund Transfer Act (Title IX of the Consumer Credit Protection Act) provides consumer protection when using a debit card or electronic means to debit or credit an

account. It limits a consumer's liability for unauthorized electronic fund transfers. The Act also establishes the rights, liabilities, and responsibilities of participants in electronic fund transfer systems. It requires all financial institutions to have in-place policies regarding transaction accounting, preauthorized transfers and error resolution. Additionally, it sets liability limits for losses as a result of *unauthorized* transfers. For a full description of this act and its provisions visit the FTC website.

The Gramm-Leach-Bliley Act also known as The Federal Financial Services Act (Brief Overview)

This act requires that financial institutions provide privacy notices to their customers, and, in certain circumstances, provide them with the opportunity to *opt-out* of disclosures of nonpublic personal information to unaffiliated third parties. This law says that financial institutions such as banks, credit unions, insurance and investment companies cannot sell your nonpublic personal information to *unaffiliated third parties* without your consent.

Such institutions must give notice of their privacy policies to their customers at least annually. Before disclosing any consumer's personal financial information to an *unaffiliated third party*, they must give the consumer the privacy policy notice and an opportunity for that consumer to "opt-out" from such disclosure. The act also limits the sharing of account number information for marketing purposes. Among other things, this law also makes it illegal for anyone to use forged, fictitious, fraudulent, and stolen documents to obtain information from any financial institution or from a customer of a financial institution.

The Credit Repair Organization Act (Brief Overview)

The Credit Repair Organization Act of 1996, amending title IV of the Consumer Credit Protection Act, prohibits untrue or misleading representations and requires certain affirmative disclosures in the offering or sale of "credit repair services." The Act bars *credit repair companies* from demanding advance payment, requires that *credit repair contracts* be in writing, and gives consumers certain contract cancellation rights. Everyone should be cautious when dealing with these organizations. *Make sure you are dealing with legitimate credit counseling services.* Remember that if you have inaccurate or incorrect information appearing on credit reports as a result of fraudulent activity, YOU DO NOT NEED A CREDIT REPAIR SERVICE. You do not need your credit repaired. You need the inaccurate information investigated and corrected or removed. You have that right under the Fair Credit Reporting Act.

Chapter 15

Important Organizations and Contacts

- Federal Trade Commission IDTheft Hotline 877-ID THEFT (877-438-4338)
- Federal Trade Commission www.consumer.gov/idtheft
- Identity Theft Management: 1-800-329-4440 www.identitytheftmanagement.com
- Social Security Administration: Fraud: 800-269-0271 www.ssa.gov
- Medicaid Fraud 1-800-892-0375
- Health Privacy Project, 202-687-0880 www.healthprivacy.org.
- National Fraud Information Center:1-800-876-7060 www.fraud.org
- Securities and Exchange Commission (SEC):202-942-7040 www.sec.gov
- Federal Communications Commission:888-225-5322www.fcc.gov/cqb.complaints.html
- United States Postal Inspection Service: www.usps.gov/postalinspectors

- The Three National Credit reporting agencies:

  ❖ Experian Information Solutions, Inc.
  Report **FRAUD**:1-800-311-4769
  www.experian.com
  Address to report inaccurate information and to request a Fraud Victim Statement
  **Experian often has affiliated credit reporting agencies assist with their reporting process. Your credit report may indicate an affiliated agency address to mail any inaccuracies or to request a fraud victim statement instead of the address below. The correct address should appear on your credit report. When in doubt, use the following address:

P.O. Box 596
Pittsburg, PA 15230

❖ Equifax Credit Information Services, Inc.
Report **FRAUD** 1-800-525-6285
www.equifax.com
Address to report inaccurate information and to
request a Fraud Victim Statement:
P.O. Box 740256
Atlanta, GA 30374-0256

❖ Trans Union Corporation –
Report **FRAUD**: 1-800-680-7289
www.tuc.com
Address to report inaccurate information and to
request a Fraud Victim Statement
Fraud Victim Assistance Department
P.O. Box 6790
Fullerton, CA 92834-6790

▪ OPT-OUT REQUESTS:
  ❖ To Opt-Out of the marketing mailing lists of the three
    National credit reporting agencies call:
    1-888-5OPT-OUT or 1-888-567-8688
    All three national credit reporting agencies: Experian,
    Equifax and Trans Union utilize the same number.

  ❖ To Opt-Out of many of the national direct marketing
    mailing lists, write the Direct Marketing Association
    at:
    DMA Preference Service
    P.O. Box 9008
    Farmingdale, NY 11735-9008

❖ To Opt-Out of many national telemarketer lists, write
the Direct Marketing Association at:
DMA Telephone Preference Service
P.O. Box 9014
Farmingdale, NY 11735-9014

▪ **Check Verification Companies:**
    ❖ SCAN: 1-800-262-7771
    ❖ TeleCheck: 1-800-710-9898 or
                                  927-0188
    ❖ CrossCheck: 1-707-586-0551
    ❖ Equifax Check Systems: 1-800-437-5120
    ❖ International Check Services: 1-800-526-5380

Chapter 16

Sample Letters

After reading the information contained in each chapter, I thought it might be of further help and assistance to include an overview of letter formats that you may use as a guide in developing your own letters to creditors and others. Everyone's creditor contact is based on specific and unique conditions. The formats provided are merely a suggestion or guide to use in developing and writing your own letters based on your specific situation. It is important that you read the information in the preceding chapters so you understand what and why particular documentation is recommended to accompany each letter. In addition, individual creditors may request additional documentation specific to your case of fraud. Remember to address *legal questions* to your attorney or a member of the legal profession.

1. Example of a Forgery Affidavit (Credit grantors typically furnish this)

2. Sample Letter to Credit Card Company Confirming a Lost or Stolen Credit Card

3. Sample Letter to Creditor Confirming Notification Of Unauthorized Activity On Your Credit Card Account

4. Sample Letter to a Service Company Confirming Fraudulent Account

5. Sample Letter Requesting a "Fraud Victim Statement" On Your Credit Reports

6. Sample Letter to Credit Reporting Agency Disputing Information On Credit Report

7. Sample Letter Requesting A Statement For Future Creditors When An Item On Your Credit Report Is Correct

8. Sample Letter to CRA Regarding Denial of Credit Due to Inaccurate Information Appearing On Credit Report

9. Sample Letter to Merchants Regarding Check Fraud

10. Sample Letter to Collection Agency Mailing Numerous Requests For Payment

Example of a Forgery Affidavit

The affidavit below provides you with an example of the information requested on Forgery Affidavits. The Federal Trade Commission has a standard ID Theft Affidavit available to download: www.ftc.org. The Forgery Affidavit provided by the FTC is longer and requests more information from the affiant. Each merchant or creditor may want you to complete their specific forgery affidavit, which may request different information.

Police Case #_____   # SAMPLE

Instructions:

Complete the following Forgery Affidavit in the presence of a NOTARY PUBLIC. Please return completed and notarized affidavit within 10 days. Your account may not be treated as a forgery until this document is returned.

AFFIDAVIT OF FORGERY

State of _____ County of _____

Before me, the undersigned Notary, on this day personally appeared _____ ("affiant"), whose address is _____, known to me to be the person whose signature appears below. Affiant, after having been duly sworn by me to tell the truth, states the following:

☐ I did not sign nor did I authorize anyone to sign on my behalf at any time nor was the person signing a signatory on any of my accounts.
☐ I did not authorize anyone to use my name or personal information to seek money, credit, loans, goods and/or services.
☐ I did not receive any benefit, money, goods or services as a result of the fraudulent use of my personal information and/or social security number.
☐ My personal identification (example: credit cards, birth certificate, driver license, social security number, etc.) were compromised on or about _____ (month/day/year)

144

I understand that making a false sworn statement is subject to Federal and State statutes and may be punishable by fines and/or imprisonment.

I DECLARE UNDER PENALTY OF PERJURY THAT THE FOREGOING IS TRUE AND CORRECT.

Signed and sworn to me, the undersigned authority on the ___day of _____20___.

By:_____   _____
Affiant Signature   (Print) Affiant Full Legal Name

Who has presented the following identification: _____

_____
Notary Signature and Seal

**After calling the credit card company and informing them of the lost or stolen card it is best to follow-up the telephone notification with written confirmation.
<u>**Sample Letter to Credit Card Company Confirming a Lost or Stolen Credit Card**</u>

(Put on your letterhead or stationery)
John Q. Public
P.O. Box 123
Anywhere, USA 55555
(555) 555-55555

Date:

REGISTERED MAIL

Name of Credit Card Company
Address
Address

Re: (Lost or Stolen) ABC Credit Card # XXXXXXXXXX

Dear (Credit Card Company):

    This letter serves as written confirmation of my *lost/stolen* (select the action that applies) (ABC credit card), reported to you on (specify date you notified creditor by phone). In accordance with my request and confirmed by your customer service representative (i.e. Lisa Lane), the account was closed/cancelled (select one) on (specify date you notified them).

Identity Fraud Victim:	John Q Public
Social Security Number	123-45-6789
Account in the name of:	John Public
Fraudulent Account Number:	# XXXXX XX XXXX
Credit Card Company	ABC Credit Card Company
Company Representative:	Lisa Lane
Police Case number:	# 4567

Detective & phone number: Det. Joe Jones, Any town Police
                              Department
                              (555) 555-1234 Ext. 45
Forgery Affidavit: Enclosed

I accept no responsibility for the account specified above. Please mail *written* confirmation of the account's closed status. Additionally, I appreciate your notifying the three national credit reporting agencies, Experian, Equifax and Trans Union, that the account has been closed by consumer. I will contact them within 30 days to confirm the closed status of the account. Should you have any questions, you may contact me at the phone number listed above. Thank you for your prompt assistance and attention to this matter.

Very truly yours,

John Q. Public

Enclosure: Affidavit of Forgery
**THIS DOCUMENT CONTAINS NONPUBLIC PERSONAL
INFORMATION.
SHRED BEFORE DISCARDING**

Sample Letter to Creditor Confirming Notification Of Unauthorized Activity

(Put on your letterhead or stationery)
John Q Public
P.O. Box 123
Anywhere, USA 55555
(555) 555-55555

Date

REGISTERED MAIL

Name of Credit Card Company
Address
Address

Re: **Unauthorized Activity On Credit Card Account #: XXXXXXXXXXX**

Dear (Credit Card Company):

This letter serves as written confirmation of our telephone conversation of (date you notified creditor to close account). I am a victim of identity theft. As previously reported to (name of credit card company), my (name of credit card and account number) was used fraudulently by persons unknown to me. I have attached a copy of my last statement dated (date of statement) and have highlighted the unauthorized activity. Pursuant to my request and confirmed by your (customer service representative or fraud investigator, Lisa Lane), the account was closed immediately. The compromised account information is listed below:

Identity Fraud Victim:	John Q Public
Social Security Number	123-45-6789
Account in the name of:	John Public
Fraudulent Account Number:	# XXXXX XX XXXX
ABC Credit Card Company Rep.	Lisa Lane
Police Case number:	# 4567

Detective & phone number:	Det. Joe Jones, Any town Police Department (555) 555-1234 Ext. 45
Forgery Affidavit:	Enclosed (Optional –They may send you one by return mail).
ABC Credit Card Co. Statement:	Enclosed –Fraudulent Activity is Highlighted

I accept no responsibility for the account specified above. Please send *written* confirmation of the accounts closing by return mail. Additionally, I appreciate your notifying the three national credit reporting agencies, Experian, Equifax and Trans Union, that the account has been closed due to fraud. I will contact them within 30 days to confirm the closed status of the account. Should you have any questions, you may contact me at the phone number listed above. Thank you for your prompt assistance and attention to this matter.

Very truly yours,

Enclosure: Billing Statement Dated (Date of attached statement)
                Affidavit of Forgery (Optional)

Sample Letter to a Service Company Confirming Fraudulent Account

(Put on your letterhead or stationery)
John Q Public
P.O. Box 123
Anywhere, USA 55555
(555) 555-55555

Date

REGISTERED MAIL

Name of Creditor
Address
Address

Re: **Notification of Fraudulent Activity on Account #: 1234**

Dear Company Name: (example: ABC Telephone Company)

This letter serves as written confirmation that (account # 1234), granted by (ABC Telephone Company) and opened in the name of (your name) is a fraudulent account. I have not authorized (ABC Telephone Company) or any of its affiliates to extend credit or services in my name. I have not opened nor have I authorized anyone else to open an account with (ABC Telephone Company) in my name or under my social security number. According to my telephone conversation with your (Customer Service Manager, Mr. Bill Smith), fraudulent account # 1234 was closed on (date of your phone call).

I accept no responsibility for account #1234. Any service (ABC Telephone Company), extended under fraudulent account # 1234 is the responsibility of (ABC Telephone Company).

The following information is provided to you as evidence of fraudulent activity perpetrated against me and in my good name.

150

Identity Fraud Victim: John Q Public
Social Security Number   123-45-6789
Account in the name of: J. Q. Public
Fraudulent Account Number: # 1234
ABC Telephone Co. Cust. Svc. Rep   Bill Smith
Police Case number: # 4567
Detective & phone number: Det. Joe Jones, Any town Police
                                                                       Department
                                                                       (555) 555-1234 Ext. 45
Forgery Affidavit: Enclosed (Optional –They may
                                                                       send you one by return mail).
ABC Tel. Co. Statement.   Enclosed –Fraudulent Activity is
                                                                       Highlighted

Should you need to speak with me personally, I may be reached during business hours at 555-555-5555 or at home at the phone number referenced above. I appreciate written confirmation of the account's cancellation by return mail. Thank you.

Very truly yours,

encl. Forgery Affidavit
ABC Telephone Co. Statement

Sample Letter Requesting a "Fraud Victim Statement" On Your Credit Reports

(Put on your letterhead or stationery)
John Q Public
P.O. Box 123
Anywhere, USA 55555
(555) 555-55555

Date

REGISTERED MAIL

Name of Credit Reporting Agency (i.e. Experian)
Address
Address

Re: **Request For A Fraud Victim Statement Added To My Credit Report**
   (Name of Agency) File Number: 123456789

Dear (Credit Reporting Agency Name):

I would like to add a fraud victim statement to my credit file with (name of credit reporting agency). I understand that this statement will remain on my credit file for 7 years.
Statement:
I am a fraud victim. I request all credit grantors contact me by phone at (555) 555-5555 before granting credit of any kind.

The following personally identifiable information is solely furnished to provide the required information and documentation to grant my fraud victim statement request.

❖ Your full and complete Name (include middle initial or if you use Jr., Sr., III, etc.)

❖ Present and previous addresses for the past five years:

1999 to Present: ABC Lane, Anywhere City, Anywhere State 55501
1996 to 1999: XYZ Road, Everywhere City, Everywhere State 55502

❖ Your Social Security Number:

❖ Date of Birth:

❖ Spouse: His/Her Name   Social Security #:

❖ Attached please find a copy of the first page of my telephone bill indicating my name, address and telephone number.

Please add my 7 year fraud victim's statement to my credit file immediately and mail me confirmation that my request as been made. I can be contacted at the phone number above, should there be any problem completing my request. Thank you.

Very truly yours,
Enclosure: Telephone bill dated:
**THIS DOCUMENT CONTAINS NONPUBLIC PERSONAL INFORMATION.
SHRED BEFORE DISCARDING**

Some credit reporting agencies include a form with your credit report enabling you to notify them of any inaccurate information appearing on your credit report. Complete and mail the form for their prompt investigation. If no form is available, this letter may be used as a guide to request the credit reporting agency investigate unauthorized information.

Sample Letter to Credit Reporting Agency
Disputing Information Appearing On Credit Report
Date

REGISTERED MAIL

Name of Credit Reporting Agency (example: Experian)
Address

Re: **Disputed item on Credit Report #: 12345**

> Your Name
> Your Address
> Your City, State, Zip
> Your Social Security #
> Your phone number

Dear Name of Credit Reporting Agency (example: Experian)

Enclosed please find a copy of my (i.e. Experian) credit report dated (date of your last report). I have highlighted (i.e. two, (2)), disputed items on my report.

The items are inaccurate due to the following:

1. Disputed item #BC123456 ABC Company
Inaccurate because account # BC123456 was opened through the fraudulent use of my personal information and social security number by persons unknown to me. Enclosed find:
- Forgery affidavit,
- Copy of the police report and case number: 6011

- Copy of letter dated (i.e. 7/15/02 from creditor, ABC company confirming the fraudulent account and its subsequent closing due to fraud

2. Disputed item #AC55555-5555 ABC Credit Card Company

Inaccurate because the ABC credit card account #AC55555-5555 was opened through the fraudulent use of my personal information and social security number. <u>Enclosed find</u>:

- A copy of letter dated (i.e.7/05/02) from creditor, (i.e. ABC Credit Card Company), confirming the fraudulent ABC Credit Card account # 55555-5555
- Copy of notarized ABC Credit Card Company forgery affidavit and referencing police case # 6011

I request that you investigate the inaccuracies stated above and delete them from appearing on my report as soon as possible. I look forward to receiving a written report of your investigation along with a copy of my corrected credit report. Should you require any additional information to remove these two inaccuracies, I may be contacted at the phone number above. Thank you for your time and consideration.

Enclosures: (5)
o Forgery affidavit -2
o police report /case number
o Creditor letters (2)

Notation: If an item on your credit report is correct but there are extenuating circumstances that you would like to explain to *future* creditors, consider using the format below in developing your own letter. Extenuating circumstances might include incidents such as an account labeled late due to an unexpected job lay-off, unexpected medical bills, credit problems as a result of divorce, etc. A brief statement of explanation may be included in your credit file. I do mean BRIEF. If it is too long, it will not be considered. (Some states have specific restrictions or allowances as to how long the explanation can be).

Sample Letter Requesting a Statement for Future Creditors Clarifying an Item on Your Credit Report (even though it is Correct)

(Put on your letterhead or stationery)
John Q Public
P.O. Box 123
Anywhere, USA 55555
(555) 555-55555

Date

REGISTERED MAIL

Name of Credit Reporting Agency
Address
Address

Re: **Credit Report Explanation Statement**

Dear Credit Reporting Agency (i.e. Experian):

Please add the following statement to my credit file pursuant to the terms setforth by (name of credit reporting agency) for brief statements of explanation.

Your Name:
Your Address:

Your Social Security #:

Account #:12121112 was late on a number of occasions due to an unexpected lay-off with my employer, (i.e. ABC Airlines). I have since paid off the account in full.

I would appreciate a copy of my amended report showing my explanation statement as soon as possible. Thank you for your time and consideration.

Very truly yours,

John Q Public

**THIS DOCUMENT CONTAINS SENSITIVE NONPUBLIC
PERSONAL INFORMATION.
SHRED BEFORE DISCARDING**

Notation: It is easier and faster to telephone the credit reporting agencies when you want a copy of your credit report because you were denied credit due to something contained within your file. The following guide is provided should you wish to document your request.

Sample Letter to Credit Reporting Agency Regarding Denial of Credit Due to Inaccurate Information Appearing On Credit Report

(Put on your letterhead)
John Q Public
P.O. Box 123
Anywhere, USA 55555

Date

REGISTERED MAIL

Name of Credit Reporting Agency
Address
Address

Re: **Denial of Credit due to Inaccurate Information Appearing on Credit Report**

Your Name
Address
SS#:
Phone Number

Dear Name of Credit Reporting Agency:

I was notified by (name of company) on (date) that my application for credit was denied due to information appearing on my credit report. Enclosed please find a copy of the notice. I believe my credit report to be *inaccurate*. Pursuant to the Fair Credit Reporting Act, please mail me a copy of my current credit report so I may correct any inaccuracies or incomplete information contained therein.

I understand that there will be no charge for the copy of my report.

Should you need to reach me during daytime business hours, I may be contacted at (555) 555-55555. Thank you for your prompt attention and assistance in forwarding my report as soon as possible.

Very truly yours,

John Q Public
enclosure: Notification of Credit Denial

**THIS DOCUMENT CONTAINS SENSITIVE PERSONAL INFORMATION.
SHRED BEFORE DISCARDING**

<u>Sample Letter to Merchants Regarding Check Fraud</u>

John Q Public
P.O. Box 123
Anywhere, USA 55555
(555) 555-55555

Date

REGISTERED MAIL

Merchant Company Name
Address
Address

Re: **Check Fraud Notification**

Dear Name of Company: (example: ABC Company)

I am in receipt of your letter dated (i.e. January XX, 2002) requesting payment in the amount of (example: $242.00). I am an identity theft victim. You are hereby notified that checking account # XXXXXXX-XXXXX is closed due to fraud. The check accepted by (ABC Company) in the amount of $242.00 was fraudulent.

I have attached a copy of the Forgery Affidavit pertaining to this account as well as pertinent information establishing fraud as it relates to checking account number XXXXXXX-XXXXX in the name of (John Q. Public).

Account Holder Name:	John Q Public
Fraudulent Account Number:	# XXXXX XX XXXX
Financial Institution:	ABC Credit Union
Financial Institution Contact Person:	Mary Smith
	800-123-1234 Ext. 123
Official Police Department Case Number:	# 4567
Investigating Detective & phone number:	Det. Joe Jones, Any town Police Department (123) 555-5555
Forgery Affidavit:	Enclosed

Credit Union Investigative Report   Enclosed

Should ABC Company receive additional checks drawn on the above account, please call Detective (Joe Jones) at the number above or your check verification company. The check verification companies have been supplied with the fraudulent account information.

Please furnish this information to the appropriate departments within your organization to pursue this matter as a fraudulent account. After having supplied ABC Company with timely information on the fraudulent checking account above, I do not expect to receive further requests for payment on this account nor should false or misleading information about me be supplied to any collection agency or credit reporting agency in association with this fraudulent checking account.

Should you wish to contact me regarding this information, I may be reached at the number printed above. Thank you for your immediate attention.

Very truly yours,
enclosures: Forgery Affidavit
        Copy of Financial Institution Official Investigation and Report

Mail the letter below to an **actual person** within the collection agency's organization. Make sure you can provide your supporting documentation of account status along with enough information to substantiate your underlying claim of undue harassment. This should assist in stopping future correspondence.

<u>Sample Letter to Collection Agency Mailing Numerous Requests for Payment</u>
<u>(After You Have Established Fraudulent Account Status)</u>

(Put on your letterhead or stationery)
John Q Public
P.O. Box 123
Anywhere, USA 55555

Date

REGISTERED MAIL

Employee's Name
Name of Collection Agency
Address
Address

Dear Mr.(Employee Name):

I am in receipt of the third letter your agency has sent me requesting payment for account # 12345.

I have furnished the necessary documentation for you to verify the debt and account #12345 as a fraudulent account on two prior occasions. I have again provided the fraudulent account information. In addition, I am furnishing the company you represent, the Credit Grantor, (ABC Credit Company), with a copy of this letter. I have given you and (ABC Collection Agency) sufficient information to <u>investigate</u> and verify the debt, account #12345, as fraudulent. I request my undue harassment by ABC Collection Agency cease. I look forward to you verifying the debt as a fraudulent account. Should I receive a fourth notice from (ABC Collection Agency), I shall seek assistance under the terms provided me by The Fair Debt Collection Practices Act.

Debt in the name of:	John Q. Public
Fraudulent Account Number:	# 1234
Police Case number:	# 4567
Detective & phone number:	Det. Joe Jones, Any town Police Department
	555) 555-1234 Ext. 45
FTC Forgery Affidavit:	Enclosed (
ABC Collection's Forgery Affidavit	Enclosed

I appreciate your immediate assistance in resolving the present situation. Thank you.

Very truly yours,

Enclosures: Copy of Previously delivered REGISTERED MAIL#1234
Copy of Previously delivered REGISTERED MAIL # 5678
FTC Forgery Affidavit
(ABC Collection Agency) Forgery Affidavit
Copy of letter to (ABC Credit Company)

Conclusion

By the end of this book, I hope that both your thinking and your behavior have changed! You may not consciously even realize it yet. You now have the power to tackle any problem you encounter proactively and not defensively. Through knowledge, persistence and perseverance, you will no longer let potential problems make you feel vulnerable. Your identity theft no longer overwhelms you. You are not only the CEO of protecting your personal information and in proving your victim status in the effort to reclaim your identity, but the CEO of your life! YOU are responsible for understanding the world as it is today. With a better understanding of how particular areas directly impact your life, you are better equipped to act in your best interest. You have learned to question *why* when the convenience of others makes you feel exposed and unsafe. *You* are in charge of *you*.

You must always remember that in the world we live in today, keeping your personal information private is a concept and no longer a reality. The potentially devastating repercussions of having your personal information compromised should be a driving force in trying to protect it as much as possible. And although nothing is foolproof, only you can allow yourself to "feel" victimized. By staying informed, aware of the logical strategies available and proactive, you begin to turn agony into answers…and your trauma into triumph!

About the Author

LouAnn Busch-White has worked with victims of identity theft since 1997. After successfully overcoming her own identity theft, LouAnn's frustration regarding limited answers and *real* assistance for identity theft victims led to her entrepreneurial mission. She founded Identity Theft Management™, a victim's advocate and identity theft consulting company specializing in assisting victims with their specific identity theft issues and circumstances and providing knowledge, direction, support and confidential assistance to *INDIVIDUAL* identity theft victims who must prove their innocence and victim status regarding fraudulent claims, acts and activity performed in their name.

LouAnn and her company have appeared frequently in nationally syndicated newspapers, national and local television and are recipients of the prestigious Oprah Winfrey owned Oxygen Media business grant award. She actively supports social security number privacy legislation on both local and federal levels and is passionate about helping the more than 800,000 annual victims of identity theft. For more information about the author and her company, please visit www.identitytheftmanagement.com

www.ingramcontent.com/pod-product-compliance
Lightning Source LLC
Chambersburg PA
CBHW020418290526
45785CB00002B/615